Sunday Worship In Your Parish

What It Is
What It Could Be

Michael J. Henchal

TWENTY-THIRD PUBLICATIONS
P.O. Box 180 West Mystic, Ct. 06388

Dedication

To my mother and father:
First teachers in the ways of faith, they have also been the best of teachers.

Acknowledgments

I want to thank everyone who helped me get these ideas into print. Friends and teachers at The Catholic University of America, Washington, D.C., provided much of the intellectual stimulus. Mr. Henry Gosselin and Miss Yvonne Goulet gave me my first chance to write for publication in *The Church World*. Parishioners in the various parishes in which I have served, especially St. Rose of Lima, Jay, Maine, encouraged me and spiritually supported me. Mrs. Dobie Nickless helped correct my grammar and punctuation. And Miss Bonnie Beaudette helped make the final corrections and assemble the material.

Nihil Obstat: Rev. James E. Connor

Imprimatur: +Edward C. O'Leary
Bishop of Portland
November 28, 1979

Edited by Marie McIntyre
Cover design by Rose Virginia DeMarco

©Copyright 1980 by Michael J. Henchal. All rights reserved. No part of this book may be reproduced in any manner without permission of the publisher. For such permission, write: Twenty-Third Publications, P.O. Box 180, West Mystic, Ct. 06388.

Library of Congress Catalog Card Number: 79-92693

ISBN 0-89622-117-2

Contents

Introduction 8

Part 1: Background

1. Back to Roots 11
2. The Ordinariness of the Task 14
3. Origins of the Mass 17
4. The Primitive Eucharist 20
5. God's Presence in Sacraments 23
6. Stop Pretending 26
7. Too Ordinary? 29

Part II: The Celebration

8. Beginning 33
9. Celebration of the Word 36
10. Preparation of the Altar and Gifts 39
11. The Eucharistic Prayer 42
12. The Communion Rite 45
13. The Silent Times 48

Part III: Ourselves

14. Our Prayer 52
15. Our Community Life 55
16. Our Preparation 57
17. Our Hospitality 60

Part IV: Conditions for Good Worship

18. Ministers of Hospitality 64
19. Ministering in Many Ways 67
20. Memories of Music 70
21. Ministry of Music 73
22. The Rhythm of Worship 76
23. Environment and Worship 79
24. Our Food for Worship 82

Conclusion: The Future 85

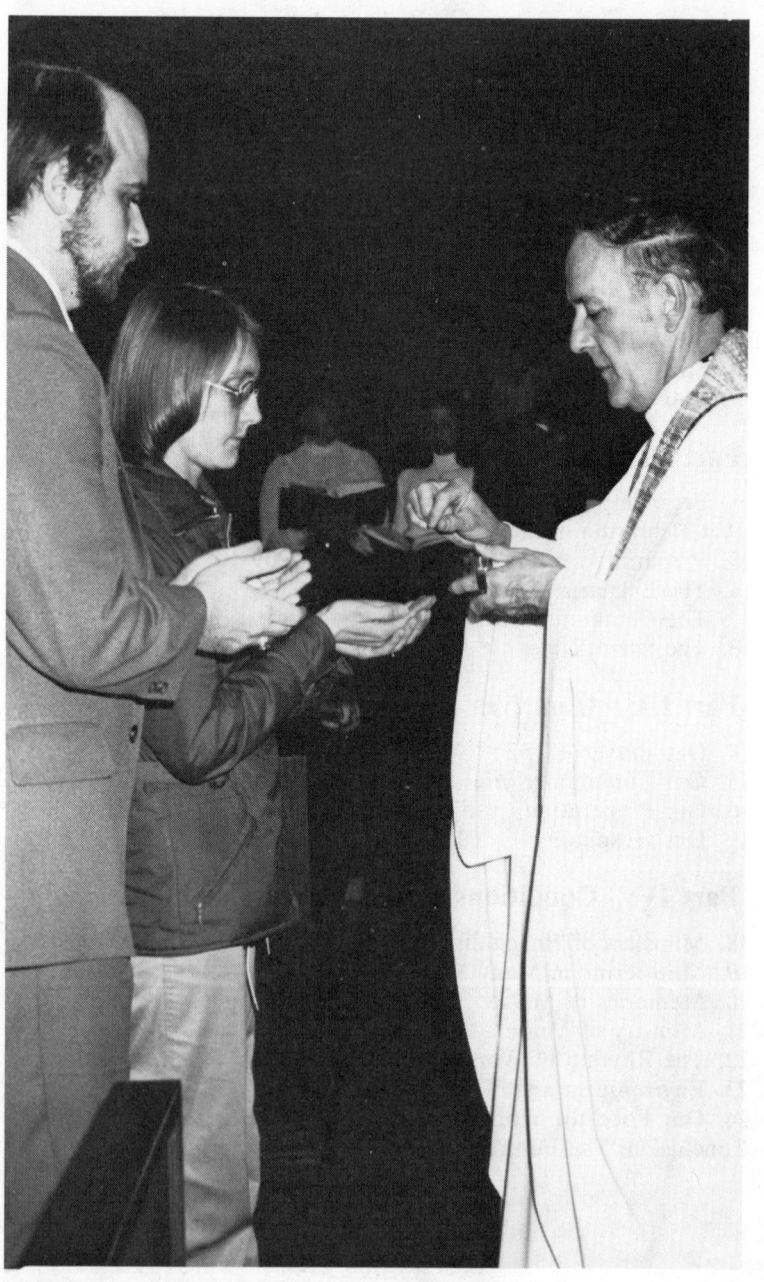

Foreword

Since Vatican Council II called for many liturgical changes almost twenty years ago, the big question that people had every right to ask, but which went pretty much unanswered, was, "Why these changes?" That was and still is one of the main reasons for the resentment and confusion we see. When people know why they are asked to change, they tend to be more willing to do so. All in all, we did a pretty bad job in helping people understand the reasons for the changes.

This situation has changed. We are, all of us, in a much better position to know why changes in the liturgy occur. But we are still not doing enough about it. As a result, people are becoming used to changes, and gradually shifting from one "routine" to another, but they are not getting the life-giving part of the renewal.

In this regard, Father Mike Henchal's book is exactly on target. It is for people in the parish, directed to those who go to Mass on Sunday. It is not a book by a liturgist for other liturgists, or for people who have a liturgical or theological background. We have many such books but only a very few people read them. Father Henchal offers to priests and parishioners alike the kind of material that should be part of Sunday preaching everywhere. In doing this service he is carrying out the most important part of his ministry as a diocesan liturgy person. The diocese sent him off to study liturgy so that he could come back and help people in parishes worship better. In this book he is doing just that. He is sharing in a very practical way all the "goodies" he discovered in his studies. Would that more diocesan liturgy persons would do the same!

Father Henchal shares two kinds of "goodies" in this book: historical background and practical suggestions. Of the two I would say that the more important is the historical background.

We came into the twentieth century thinking that our liturgy was unchangeable. This was perhaps the greatest barrier to a wider acceptance of liturgical change. The mere suggestion of change was an affront to basic attitudes that were more than four hundred years old: "Ritual actions must be the same everywhere." "Nothing is to be changed." Stern and unyielding "rubrics" wielded their impersonal power over all saying and singing of Mass. The word "celebration" was hardly used, let alone understood. We "went" to Mass; we "heard" Mass. The priest was the only minister and he "said" Mass. The Latin tongue held unquestioned sway in the world of sacraments. I can remember when we were practically forbidden even to talk about the possibility of the vernacular. Because we did not know our history, we thought that's the way it always was and always should be.

We know now that it was just the opposite. The history of church and sacraments is altogether a history of change, lots of change. History tells us that change is the necessary life-energy of church and sacrament. Father Henchal's book can help a lot of people begin to understand this fact. He offers valuable insights into the history of liturgical change. And he offers these insights in a way that people can get hold of.

The rest of this book is very practical, lots of practical suggestions for worshiping better. I would hope that priests would preach these insights at Sunday Mass. That's the only place most people get a chance to hear about them. I would hope that liturgy committees and church ministers would get hold of them, share them, and do something about them. I would hope that religious educators and families would use the book. I would hope that more "liturgists" will offer this kind of plain fare to people who so badly need to understand and want to understand.

        Eugene A. Walsh, S.S.
        Catholic University of America
        December 26, 1979

Introduction

Effective worship has the power to transform all of life. It can serve as the source of and the impetus behind all parish activity, the summit of all our meetings and classes, and the counselling and care for the poor and the sick. I want parishes to be centers of spirituality, places of prayer and conversion, where you come to learn to pray, to pray, and to grow in your spiritual life.

For many years now if you wanted to encounter God, enrich your spiritual life, learn how to pray, or know Jesus as the personal center of your life, you went away from the parish to a retreat house far from home or took part in one of several weekend "encounters" provided by the different movements. For many years, parishes have been the places you left to find God, when they should be the most common meeting ground with God. And within the parish, among its activities, the central meeting ground ought to be the Sunday Eucharist.

But I don't see this happening in very many parishes. Many seem to have forgotten a very important law: "Good celebrations foster and nourish faith. Poor celebrations weaken and destroy faith" (Bishops' Committee on the Liturgy, *Music in Catholic Worship*).

Father Eugene Walsh of The Catholic University of America, to whom I acknowledge a great debt, said it somewhat like this: If one weekend you are invited to a party where the food is bad, the booze is cheap, or there is none at all, the music is lousy, there is no singing or dancing, most of the people are strangers, no one bothers to introduce you, the host does all the talking, and says nothing of interest, you go home. And, if the following week you are invited back again, do you go?

Of course not. And yet that's exactly what we do in some parishes, week after week, and we wonder why they're not coming to church as they used to. On top of all that, many of those who do come pass the time with that glazed look in their eyes, cleaning their fingernails, coughing, squirming, and reading the bulletin. They come late and leave early and sit back far enough so they don't have to get involved.

That may sound overly pessimistic to you. If I sound that way at times, it is only because I have such an exciting image of what it is supposed to be like.

It has to be better than it is. And it must be in the parish and at the Sunday Eucharist.

There's a good statistical reason why this has to be so: only a small minority in even the most active parish will ever take the opportunity to go outside the parish to "find God." The largest percentage of parishioners remain unevangelized and unprepared for the responsibilities of caring for the church demanded in the post-Vatican II era.

There are theological reasons, too: it has to do with what it means to be a local church. It also has to do with our understanding of God (you don't have to go out to the desert to find him; he is closer to home). It has to do with the meaning of the Incarnation (the Word became flesh, incarnate in daily life).

I really believe that if we can earnestly mean the words and gestures that we rehearse each Sunday, our worship will be effective, and our Sunday assemblies will be filled, instead of with boredom, "with every grace and blessing through Christ our Lord" (from the first Eucharistic Prayer).

PART I
BACKGROUND

1. Back to Roots

I am, like many liturgists, a fervent traditionalist. Please note that not everything that is old is traditional. Wearing my grandfather's hat would not be traditional. Let me explain what I mean:

For several hundred years — from roughly the 12th to the 20th centuries — few people received communion more than once a year. St. Pius X, at the turn of the century, began encouraging frequent, even daily communion, in direct opposition to the existing, longstanding situation. Who was traditional? Note that the pope was being consistent with the teachings of the earliest centuries of the church's history, as found in the works of St. Ambrose, Hippolytus, and Tertullian. Infrequent communion, I think you will agree, is not traditional, though very old. Infrequent communion represents a loss of understanding and of normal and healthy development in the life of the church.

What, then, of the Tridentine Mass, the form of the Mass first authorized by Pope Pius V in 1570? Some go as far as to say that the old form is traditional while the form authorized by the Vatican Council II and Pope Paul VI is new, untraditional, and irresponsible.

What was this "old" Mass? Pius V authorized it in 1570 in order, he tells us in the foreword to his missal, to restore the rites to the pristine, clear, simple, and vigorous, form that was known in the days of the early Fathers. To accomplish this task, he set up a commission of experts who had searched the Vatican libraries for manuscripts and other historical evidence, and their product was the Missal of Pius V, which continued in use, virtually unchanged, for 400 years.

Please note what he himself says was his aim, "to restore the rites to their pristine form." Now his scholars had a very hard time. Historical research was almost impossible at that time, a time even more confused than the present age. The best that researchers could hope to do was restore the liturgy to the form it had had under Pope Gregory VII, who died in 1085. They knew nothing of the liturgy of the Fathers.

Historical studies, as a real science, only began in the last couple of centuries. Only in the last 100 years have we been able to say with any certainty what the pristine liturgy of the Fathers looked like. The results of these historical studies show that the liturgy of Gregory VII (hence the "ideal," they thought, in 1570) is hardly ideal at all.

Pope St. Pius X, at the turn of the century, began putting this new knowledge to use. He encouraged frequent communion, as we have already seen, and he began to restore church music and to clear up the horribly cluttered church calendar and the divine office. Pius XII continued that work and also made a clarion call for active and full participation in the liturgy by all the people. He revised almost entirely, as the result of historical studies, the rites of Holy Week, and encouraged theological and liturgical studies of the Mass.

Then came the Vatican Council II. All of the scholars (in some ways I would say the sons of the scholars that Pius V had set to work 400 years earlier) came with their new insights — old insights, actually, lost and now found. The product of that Council was the missal of Paul VI in 1970. The goal set by Pius V 400 years earlier was now able to be accomplished and we, today, press forward toward the fulfillment of his dream, that the liturgy be fully restored to the pristine vigor of the early Fathers.

Who, then, is the rightful heir of Pius V, indeed, of tradition? Is it the one who clings to a liturgy which was only the imperfect product of a very restricted age, or the one who sets as his standard the goal of Pius V, incorporating the accumulated wisdom of the ages? Who is the true traditionalist?

2. The Ordinariness of the Task

Father Robert Hovda once gave a talk in which he described what he calls the "seven capital feelings" that a parish liturgy committee should have in order to carry out its tasks. The very first of these he calls a sense of "the ordinariness of the task." I like that and I would like to draw out the implications of that phrase as we examine together the meaning of the Eucharist.

My experience tells me that we usually approach any active, ecclesial role with an extreme sense of inadequacy, unworthiness, and guilt. Something in the spirituality that has been drummed into us tells us that we should feel good when we feel bad and feel bad when we feel good. We have been conditioned to believe ourselves to be incapable of handling the church's (our Father's) business. And, lest we forget that lesson, we are constantly reminded that (unless we are priests or religious brothers or sisters) we are "lay persons." And, whatever that word is supposed to mean, what it actually means in today's parlance is that we "don't know what the heck is going on." A "layman" is someone who doesn't know what he is doing. In that sense of the word, there are no lay persons in the church. Active, ecclesial roles are exactly what have been entrusted to us by our Baptism, Confirmation and first Eucharist.

A most consistent enemy of Christianity since the very first century, when Simon Magus tried to buy the secrets of the Kingdom from Peter, has been gnosticism. Gnosticism is the heresy that believes there is a secret body of wisdom, unraveling the mysteries of the universe, that only a very few initiates can share. Christianity believes, on the contrary, that the mysteries are unveiled for all the baptized and that Baptism is available to everyone, free.

But Americans find that so hard to believe. It is a basic element in American philosophy that there is no such thing as a free lunch. We would rather believe that salvation comes to those who work hardest to untangle complicated puzzles and to master intricate systems, than believe it comes freely and equally to all who call upon God in faith.

We want to believe that there are specialists with stores of secret knowledge out there who alone can make liturgy beautiful and meaningful. Yet, the only requirement mentioned anywhere in official documents of the church for full, conscious, and active participation and co-offering of the Eucharist with the priest is Baptism, Confirmation and first Eucharist. There are no further mysteries into which we must be initiated. *Worship is the most ordinary and most natural act of a Christian. We have made it unnecessarily complicated.*

Simple first-century fishermen, probably uneducated, put the thing together in the first place and transmitted their experience to many others without too much difficulty. St. Augustine told his congregation in North Africa in the fifth century that the rites of Christianity are "easy to understand . . . easy to celebrate."

Now, you have a right to ask, if this is all so easy to understand and celebrate, then why are you buying and reading a book about it and why does it seem so complicated and unnatural? I'll let Professor Balthasar Fischer of the Liturgical Institute of Trier, Germany, try to explain it:

> When a person has been in a cast for a long time, and then one day the cast is removed, he realizes that at

last he is back to his natural condition. Nevertheless, in the beginning he feels a little ill at ease and awkward. In a sense, the same will be true of the faithful with the reform of the liturgy. . . . But very soon the conviction and the feeling that one is returning to a natural state that had been forgotten will prevail. What was stiff and formal will become natural and easy, for that is what happens when normal conditions are reached.

Just a little history and little explanation and you will be able to see how natural the Mass is and how easy it is to use the forms and structures of the Mass effectively in your own parish.

3. Origins of the Mass

To understand the Eucharist, it is important to understand its source. Everyone knows it comes from the Last Supper that Jesus shared with his disciples before his death on the cross. Shouldn't that tell us something about what the Mass is?

For example, every so often you hear someone complain of a new church building. "It just doesn't look like a church." What does a church look like I wonder? And, wondering further, would this person have made the same complaint to Peter in the Upper Room? Maybe churches should look like dining rooms. It's worth considering.

Anyway, my point is that it is worth looking at where the Mass comes from. It has a history, after all; it did not suddenly appear from nowhere.

In the first instance, the Mass comes from the Jews, those of the first century to be more precise. Judaism of Jesus' time was not simple and uniform. There was a common nucleus of belief, but there was a multiplicity of sects, each with its own rabbi or teacher. Judaism was mostly the gathering of all these sects with all their different teachers and differing interpretations of the Law.

One of the common practices of these different teachers and sects was to gather from time to time, perhaps once a week, say, over a meal, to discuss the latest socio-political events, all under the umbrella of theological concern. The largest percentage of a teacher's work might be at these luncheon or dinner gatherings, which were not so terribly unlike modern Rotary or Kiwanis luncheons, though with a decidedly religious focus.

Jesus was just such a teacher, and Christianity, in the beginning, was just another (or so it appeared to be) Jewish sect. Look at the large number of times (I can count at least eight in Luke's Gospel) that Jesus is found at table, telling his stories and commenting on the times.

All Jewish meals are minor rituals. Nothing is eaten without first blessing God for it. Hors d'oeuvres might be served first, over which each guest said his own blessing. Then, there would be the washing of hands and the meal proper would begin as the host (or the teacher) would break the bread and bless it saying, "Blest are you, Lord God eternal King, who brings forth bread from the earth." He would break a piece off for each of the participants, and Jesus may well have added the words, "This is my Body, broken for you" or something like that at the Last Supper.

The main courses followed with their prescribed short blessings. At the close of the meal, hands were washed again. (If perfume were offered, it was poured into the hands of the guests, who then wiped their hands on the servant's hair!). The leader then said, "Let us give thanks," adding, if there were 100 or more present, "to the Lord our God." That should sound familiar to you. Next, there was a long three-part blessing after the meal, followed on special occasions by a glass of wine, shared by all. Again, we can imagine that at the Last Supper Jesus finished the blessings and then added, "This is the cup of my blood of the covenant." They then sang a psalm and departed.

The Last Supper may or may not have been a Passover meal (John says it was not, the other Gospels seem to say it was; scholars are divided). It scarcely matters, since the outline I have just sketched applies in any case, the prayers were merely a bit more complex on Passover.

Whatever the command, "Do this in memory of me,"

means, it does not mean, "Gather and give thanks, break bread and share a cup of wine." People in Jewish society would have done that without being told. What Jesus commanded was to do it "in memory of me." Therefore, when they gathered for their weekly luncheon or dinner, they remembered him and all the times before when he had broken the bread and said the blessing and shared his insights with them. Remembering him, they were conscious that he was with them still, especially and marvelously as a fellow participant at their table, sharing his life with them as they shared their lives with him.

So, even today we take, bless and break bread to share; take, bless, and drink of the one cup to mingle our lives together with his, recognizing the Lord Jesus "in the breaking of the bread."

4. The Primitive Eucharist

The beginnings of the Eucharist are found in the simple meals of brotherhood and sisterhood which the followers of Jesus had shared with him so often during his earthly ministry, culminating in the final meal, the Last Supper.

When Jesus was gone from their midst, it was only natural that his Jewish followers would continue to gather in private homes, private dining halls, and restaurants (Luke 24:30ff and Acts 2:46) for a common meal. Those times had been so important when they had shared them with Jesus, you might expect that, gathering now without him, these would be the times when they would miss him the most. The miracle was and continues to be that, instead of missing him the most at these gatherings, these were the times that they experienced his presence the most intensely, in the most concentrated form. They realized (made real) the Lord's presence among them in the breaking of the bread.

They continued to gather each week with their brother Jews at the synagogue until they were expelled from the synagogues. Their own service of the Word was shaped by what they saw and heard there. After explusion, the liturgy of the Word continued to be celebrated briefly in a service separate from the liturgy of the Eucharist.

The liturgy of the Eucharist was celebrated mostly in private homes, in the living rooms and dining rooms of more well-to-do Christians. The head of the local Church would sit in the great chair, probably not unlike the one your father and mine sit in each evening to read the paper.

It is an undisputed fact that the church architecture does not come from the design of temples or synagogues, religious buildings. Churches are rather built on the model of the contemporary Roman house, a secular building. In Rome, even today, several examples can be found of church buildings which evolved out of the homes of Christians, the remains of which serve as foundations for the later structures. (The idea that the early Christians gathered regularly in the catacombs is mostly pious, romantic nonsense. Celebration of the Eucharist in cemeteries is a comparatively late development associated with the cult of the martyrs.)

Quite early, those elements of the meal to which Jesus had drawn special attention (the breaking and sharing of bread at the beginning of the meal and the final cup of blessing) were separated from the meal proper. Reasons for this separation are obscure. Perhaps it was caused by the abuses Paul describes in Corinth. The meal, when separated from the Eucharist proper, became the meal of the community for the poor, called an agape or love feast. Food for the agape came from the food brought and presented at the offertory.

The Eucharistic prayers evolved from the great prayer of blessing that went with the final cup. Since it was so much longer and more developed than the prayer that accompanied the blessing over the bread, it became the blessing for both, once the two were combined by the elimination of the meal itself.

It would be safe to say that this primitive liturgy of the Eucharist would not have had to take more than 15-20 minutes to celebrate. During times of persecution, when it was dangerous to assemble, it probably was that short.

Quite obviously, this was a very simple and straightforward ritual. Everyone could immediately see what was going on and understand it. There was no need for commentators or explanation of the gestures. Words and gestures, though profound, were also transparent.

Can we make them transparent again today? Can our Eucharist look, feel, and sound like what it is? Why must it be so complicated?

5. God's Presence in Sacraments

We have been discussing the ordinariness of the task of worship, a phrase borrowed from Rev. Robert Hovda and then reworked. The rites of Christianity are easy to celebrate and easy to understand, as St. Augustine said. We can know what we are doing. We can do it well. We can do it better.

We have already seen that the Eucharist comes from the ordinary, frequent gatherings of the disciples with Jesus for meals, then finally the Last Meal, the Last Supper. We know that the disciples continued to gather for these meals even after the Ascension and Pentecost at which time they realized that Jesus was not absent but with them, still sharing in their meal and in their prayers and in their lives.

Something is missing from our lives lately. Experience of the holy is elusive even as we gather in our Eucharistic assemblies. God seems to be missing from much of our society and daily lives, as he also seems to be missing from the many words, gestures, noise, and moving about of our Sunday worship. How does God come to us in our community of faith anyway?

Surely God reveals himself to us through human acts. Look at the Incarnation, for example. God became man. Historically, God entered into our lives through the taking-on of human life in Jesus, through the enfleshment of the Son. In Jesus are joined inseparably the human and the divine, the highest transcendence and the closest familiarity, the sacred and the secular. Only in this way could God become fully available and accessible to humankind.

And today? Well, first of all, God is everywhere, of course, and, even further, we are the Body of Christ, the presence of God in the world in the union of the common Spirit that we share that is of God. God is still manifest in human acts, still enfleshed in human and everyday, everywhere forms.

That presence may seem too diffuse, too tenuous, almost chaotic for us to be able to gather our lives around it and draw strength from it continuously. While it remains true that we could see God through the window of every created thing, we see him better through certain acts, gestures, words and materials. These are the things of earth and the work of human hands which are the vehicles for God to enter our lives, for the self-communication of God. These are the gestures, words, acts, and materials which make, as did Jesus' humanity, grace accessible and available for us today. These make the Word which is life something we have heard, something we have seen with our own eyes, something we have watched and touched with our hands (1 John 1:1).

This is the principle of the Incarnation and, as well, the principle of the sacraments. You take some of the ordinary and place it at a distance, where it can be seen better and clearer, thus making it extra-ordinary, so that it can serve as the center around which we gather up the fragments of our broken existence, giving us shape and meaning and life, making all of life extraordinary.

Notice what we have done. We have tended to remove these acts, gestures, words, and materials so far from human and ordinary experience that we tend to forget their origins. As a result, God never quite gets enfleshed in our daily lives. We even stop looking for him there, looking, rather, only for extraordinary, miraculous ways for him to get in, vitiating the Incarnation.

For God to be a part of our experience, the vehicles of

the sacraments must come from our experience, from our lives, from our ordinary lives. Instead, we speak in our churches in an artificial, ecclesiastical prose; we sing with music that fails to be music; we share broken bread and wine, by sharing only bread, which is not broken but pre-cut and which hardly resembles bread at all. We plunge people into the mystery of Baptism with a couple drops of water from a fake seashell. Is it any wonder that God is absent from our society and our daily lives? We will not let him in.

6. Stop Pretending

The Word became flesh. We can find God in our world because he chose to put himself here. The sacraments are the continuing manifestations of God-with-us in our real, ordinary lives. For him to be found there, the words, gestures, objects, and actions of worship must clearly come from the real, ordinary world; otherwise, they cannot mediate God to our lives. This is, at once, the principle of the Incarnation and of the sacraments. The truth of worship demands that the things of worship be allowed to be what they are. Without that integrity of worship, there is no experience of the presence of God throughout our lives. We cannot just pretend.

But pretend we do. Mr. Batastini, a noted church musician, provided me with my first example of pretending in the liturgy. He tells how he visited a strange parish one week. The lector announced the hymn, the organist played the introduction, but when it came time to begin to sing, no one sang, not even a song-leader. Obviously, no one had ever heard the song before. The organist kept on playing as the celebrant entered to a chorus of nothing. He reached his chair and they pretended their way through the second verse.

The example is extreme, but haven't we all witnessed the polite, silent congregations who stand through the one verse of the final hymn, waiting to escape? Pretend music? Maybe, because it's only a pretend congregation to begin with; maybe, because it is only a pretend song;

maybe, because it is only a pretend organist being paid a pretend salary.

Next is the Eucharist itself, where we pretend to eat and drink by only eating, and, on top of that, what we receive under the species of bread, in fact, in no way resembles bread at all! Have you ever had to convince a child who was about to receive First Communion, not that after the consecration it is the Body of Christ, but that before the consecration it is bread? It looks more like styrofoam and tastes rather like it, too. It's pretend bread, of course, and we pretend again at the breaking of the bread, so that we can pretend that the sharing in the one bread joins us as one. The principle of integrity in worship tells us that bread must be bread, just as music must really be music.

There is also a great deal of pretend prayer. "Let us pray," the priest says, and pauses about three seconds, not nearly enough to begin to pray, but just long enough to pretend to. Consider the pause at the General Intercessions, to remember your private intentions in silence. Well, let me tell you, you better not have more than half a private intention, unless what you have is a long list of only pretend things about which to pray.

And the pretend words. An article I read several years ago was entitled, "From Ecclesiastical Prose, Deliver Us, O Lord." We would never use a simple sentence when we can twist and compound it, and we never use the active voice when we can use the passive one. Never say "first" when you can say "initial," or "end" when you can say "terminate," or use a noun without at least one three-syllable adjective. Always throw in words like "finalize," "objectify," "moreover," "heretofore," "feasible," "outreach," "interdependent." Say things like "transparent hearts give reflection of Tabor's light within." Use these rules, when you are only pretending to have something to say — pretend words.

We also use pretend plates for the bread, which look more like cups. We cover our candles with white metal sheaths so we can pretend they never burn down. And the height of pretend: imitation plants and flowers in the sanctuary! Reminds me of the song, "Paper Roses": "But they're only imitation, like your imitation love for me."

If a group of children wanted to play church, they couldn't find materials any less likely, any more pretend, than what we ordinarily use in our churches as the real (?) thing.

7. Too Ordinary?

We have been stressing the truth that worship must be ordinary, that is, it cannot be less human than Jesus was and he was fully and completely human. The elements of worship, then, must also be real and ordinary, never pretend. We must stop using pretend music, pretend words, pretend bread, pretend flowers, and so forth.

When I presented this opinion to a friend last summer, he objected. He said that if worship is homogeneous with life, then it no longer has the power to transform life. This objection is much the same as that of Karl Barth, a great Protestant theologian who asks "whether it is not true that when people come to worship they consciously or unconsciously leave behind the cherry tree, the symphony, the state, and their daily work as possibilities somehow exhausted?" Others, as well, indicate that the extremists who conceive of the communion service as an affair of coffee and doughnuts spiced with vague warm feelings toward one another and Jesus are seriously mistaken.

I hasten to agree: worship's task is not merely to repeat life; it must transform it. The process must be: take something of the ordinary, place it at a distance, make it extraordinary so that it can make all of life extraordinary. Note, there are two basic elements in the process of ritual: we need something of the ordinary and we must place it at a distance. My objection generally is that we fail to take something of the ordinary, but my friend is right in saying we can also fail by failing to place it at a distance. When that happens, worship and the church become little more than just another social gathering or community meeting, with speeches and refreshments and stuff.

Worship is a lot like art in this regard. The artist's task is not to reproduce exactly everything he sees. His task is to abstract from nature and create a more forceful, uncluttered statement than nature itself can make, precisely by leaving things out. So, too, in worship. The gestures and words and things can be quite abortive imitations of what they are, showing only their significant features, stripping away extraneous detail, trying to be all the more provocative, providing a more uncluttered view on the sacred that pervades all life since God poured himself into the world in the Incarnation and the Pentecost events.

Because of this, the bath of Baptism doesn't have to be a complete bath; hopefully the candidates for Baptism have already bathed. The eating and drinking of the Eucharist are not intended to supply satisfaction for physical hunger. Paul told the Corinthians, "Surely you have homes for eating and drinking." So, too, the sign of peace at Mass does not have to be so extended that it seems important or necessary to greet every member of the community or even a very large percentage. That kind of greeting is good and important (and the lack of hospitality in our churches is scandalous), but it is not good ritual action.

What am I saying? I would not support, on the grounds of the ordinariness of worship, a celebrant who walks, talks, and moves in the casual, familiar (in that sense "ordinary") way that he usually talks, moves, walks. Very few of our priests move naturally with the gracefulness and reverence that worship demands. Very few speak spontaneously in language which is sufficiently harmonious, lyrical, and poetic to carry off worship effectively. I am not calling for the use of Country Kitchen Bread, excellence of the product notwithstanding; special bread is indeed called for. When these movements, words, and things become so aborted and contracted, however, that it is no longer recognized that they come from real, ordinary life, then they are pretend and (at the opposite extreme) lose their ability to transform life.

I am calling for balance between 1) failing by not being ordinary enough — being pretend and 2) failing by being too ordinary. Worship fails for both reasons; sometimes even within the same celebration!

PART II

The Celebration

8. Beginning

"Good celebrations foster and nourish faith. Poor celebrations weaken and destroy faith." Keeping these words in mind from *Music in Catholic Worship* by the American Bishops' Committee on the Liturgy, let us look at our weekly celebrations of the Eucharist. Let's see how the parts ought to fit together in a humanly warm and divinely grace-full way.

The purpose of the entrance rites is to make a good beginning. And that's all. They are actually very little of themselves. And there is a principle in liturgy that what is important should look important and what is less important should look less important. Big things should appear big and small things small. The entrance rites are meant to be subservient to the Gospel. The Gospel is why we've come to the liturgy of the Word and so everything in the liturgy of the Word should clearly point to that good news.

You have to be careful with these entrance rites then. They can get too cumbersome. The reformed Mass is not too successful here. It is not always obvious that they are meant to make us better able to hear the good news. I mean, there are so many things: the gathering, a song, a greeting, a theme statement, a penitential rite, a hymn of praise, silence and a prayer. By the time you get through all of that, you could easily be too worn out to listen to the Word.

In the rule book, *The General Instruction*, there is an interesting statement about the beginning. It says,

"After the people have assembled. . . ." I don't think that means simply that they have been crowded into the same room. I think it means that they have passed over from being just a crowd to being a community. The most important step in preparing people to hear the Gospel is getting them assembled.

Probably the first thing necessary to assemble a group — any group — is eye contact, making a kind of spiritual rapport between, in our case, priest/celebrant and congregation and between members of the congregation as well. That may sound simplistic, but if you never catch my eye then I'll always suppose you aren't talking to me, that we aren't really present to one another, that you're talking to a booklet or the air and you don't really care about me. That being so, we'll remain apart and the Eucharist's task of making us one will have little chance.

After that bit of human contact, there are song and greeting to gather the assembly. The song gathers the group as only song can do. Many lectors and song leaders have fallen into a habit of saying that the song is "to greet our celebrant". But song is more than that. You've seen it in bars and at football games and around camp fires. Songs bring people together. Then, the word of greeting with the eye contact, when you look at each other and mean what you say, "Peace be with you" or "Grace and peace from God our Father" or even "Good morning." This greeting ought to feel and sound like a greeting, indicating that you really are glad to see me.

At this time, there is a trap set for the unwary. The liturgy is to be introduced with a few words. Very often, they become far too many words. The number of words in the introduction is inversely proportioned to the ability of people to pay attention to the Word of God. The more said before the Word, the less we may hear the Word.

The so-called Penitential Rite is another trap. It's not even traditional. The Roman Mass had no penitential formulas until the Lamb of God was introduced in the ninth century. The *Confiteor* came almost twice as late as that and it was overlaid with the singing of the *Introit* at high

Mass. The "Lord, have mercy" was originally the response to the general intercessions, moved to before the Gospel by Pope Gelasius in the late 400's. So even the "Lord, have mercy" was originally a prayer of petition and not penitential at all. So this whole penitential thing is a recent novelty. Now the examples in the sacramentary are not all that penitential really. They are certainly not little examinations of conscience. What they are, are acclamations of Christ, clearly indicating before we begin our prayer in earnest that we know that we are dependent upon God for everything we are and do. And that is a fitting step to take between greeting and Opening Prayer.

Having acknowledged our dependence on God and our own insufficiency, we call upon God in prayer, summing up, collecting all the prayer of this community at this season of their lives together.

This then is the introduction. Simple enough: personal contact, song, greeting, prayer. Passing through this vestibule, we come into the main room, the Word itself.

9. Celebration of the Word

Once we have been prepared by the introductory rites we are ready to hear the Word itself. The Word itself, like the whole of the Mass, is a living, breathing thing. Like every living thing, there is a natural rhythm to its life, characterized by successive moments of activity and rest, breathing in and breathing out, speech and silence, highs and lows. So the Liturgy of the Word is composed of different parts, serving different purposes, with different kinds of importance.

The first element is, obviously, the first reading. This is a high point, a moment of enthusiasm and tension. The Word is proclaimed by the person of faith who is giving his or her personal witness, which is at one and the same time the witness of our ancestors in the faith. Ordinarily, this reading at Sunday Masses will come from the Hebrew scriptures and has been chosen because it complements the Gospel reading.

Highs are followed by lows, breathing out with breathing in, activity by rest. So after the first reading we need a period of decreased activity, allowing us the leisure to absorb the reading we have just heard. The Church provides us with a song, the Responsorial Psalm. The psalm is meant to serve as a prayerful reflection on the reading. And, while psalms do at times contain messages of significance, the message is not exactly the point. The tone, the texture, the melody, the nonverbal elements of the Responsorial Psalm are the message.

For parish worship to work properly, we need to pay

close attention to what we are doing with this moment of rest. If the psalm is simply read it becomes just another reading. Reading piled on top of reading won't work. We have a lot of freedom here to use whichever psalm text we wish in almost whatever form will work most effectively. We have been given this freedom because the Church wants us to find ways to sing the psalm. Psalms are songs and songs must be sung or they don't work.

This bring us to the second reading. And everything we said about the first reading applies to the second, except that on Sundays this reading has not been chosen because it fits the "theme" of the Mass. These are, rather, continuous readings from the epistles; one week's reading simply picks up from where we left off the week before.

The response to the second reading is silence. A significant pause is called for, since this silence is a specific part of the Mass and not an optional "extra."

After the silence, while the priest or deacon processes solemnly to the pulpit to read the Gospel, which is the highest moment in the Liturgy of the Word, the congregation acclaims the Gospel with a kind of fanfare or flourish of trumpets, with the Alleluia. The rules say that if you can't sing the Alleluia (and I don't know why you would not be able to sing it) then it should simply be dropped. Reciting the Alleluia in any way other than song will be like reciting "Happy Birthday" when the cake is brought out of the kitchen at a birthday party.

Just a word about the homily. No longer is it to be thought of as an interruption in the order of Mass. It is an integral part of the celebration. A Mass without a homily is somehow incomplete, even a daily Mass. A Mass without a homily is as incomplete as a Mass when there would be no breaking and sharing of the bread in communion. The homily breaks open and distributes the Word. In this reflection on the Word and the liturgical year, the Word is applied to the concrete lives of the people.

We bring the Liturgy of the Word to a close with prayers for all of the world. Our reflection on God's presence through Christ and ourselves in the world has called us to take responsibility for the world. Our first response to this response-ability is going to be prayer if we are being consistent with our call. What "bad news" in your world needs to be transformed by the Gospel into "good news"? That's the question we should be asking ourselves as we compose prayers of the faithful. The principle source for intentions for the General Intercessions shouldn't be those handy, ready-made intentions in one of those "worship aids" (which are so often obstacles rather than aids). The principle source should be the newspapers, the six-o'clock news and our daily lives. We have plenty to pray about and people like to pray about things for which they feel the need. So make the General Intercessions a real response to the Word in our world today.

10. Preparation of the Altar and Gifts

The Liturgy of the Eucharist, from earliest times through all the stages of development that it has gone through to the present, has been composed of four actions: taking the bread and wine, blessing them (or giving thanks over them, which is the same), breaking the bread and giving it to all. These simple four actions are the early Church's contraction of the seven actions described in the New Testament accounts of what Jesus did at the Last Supper. There he took bread, blessed it, broke it and gave it to his disciples. Then, after they had eaten, he took a cup of wine, gave thanks and gave it to them all. Drop the meal from the middle and push the bread and wine actions together and you get the four-action shape of the Liturgy of the Eucharist, at which we will now begin to look.

If you go back to the old hand missal that you put away 15 years ago, you will find a part of the Mass called "The Offertory". Take up the sacramentary or the missalette today, turn to the same section and, search as you will, you will find no such thing. Instead, you will find The Preparation of the Altar and Gifts. So what happened? And is what happened of any significance?

When we speak of the Mass as sacrifice, we say that the gift being offered is Jesus. But clearly this doesn't happen before the Eucharistic Prayer. Rather than offering the Gift at this time, we are simply making the place, making the elements available, getting ready for the later offering.

The rite of preparation of the altar and gifts is, then, an introduction, much like the entrance rite to the Liturgy of the Word. The same rules apply as well. The reformed Mass allows this simplicity, but does not go far enough to actively encourage it. Introductory rites need to be kept brief, so as not to overshadow the more important things that follow. Make the celebration larger and you can proportionately increase the size and solemnity of the preparatory rites. I keep thinking of a lady who once told me of a Mass they had in her parish at Thanksgiving at which, she told me, the offertory procession was the "high point" of the whole celebration. What a shame, I thought. (By the way, some of the books available on children's liturgies make the same mistake.)

Take, bless, break, and give. The taking is the most practical detail which must be attended to first. We are setting the table, setting the scene for the great things which will happen next. For this action, no grand and sweeping gestures are needed.

Have an offertory procession, if you wish, although there is something artificial (not to say pretend) about having people bring up the gifts that we took out of the sacristy and carried down to the entrance in the first place. How much better if people brought their own, homemade bread and a bottle of wine with them to present at this time. Then they could really feel that this is their gift. Bring up other things at this time, if you insist, but make it visually and ritually clear that the bread and wine are the most significant, most meaningful gifts presented.

The old vocabulary, "offertory," is not without all value. For while this is not the offertory of the Gift, it is not without significance.

Everything belongs to God and comes forth from him and returns to him, even ourselves. Once in a while, we need to acknowledge this ultimate dependence on God. So we take something of the ordinary and set it apart, maybe up on a pedestal, so we can look at it more closely, in isolation. And, when we do, we see through its ordinariness to the extraordinary nature of its being from and unto God. When we do this with some of the ordinary, some of this newfound extraordinariness flows back on every other ordinary thing, ourselves included.

This process, then, of setting aside, is the first step toward the linking of this thing and then all things to Christ. It is an opening up so that Christ can enter in, an opening up not only of bread or wine but of ourselves. In some sense you might want to call this an offering for the coming epiphany, the manifestation of God incarnate.

It can be done very simply. No overwhelming need for song or even spoken word. Better to simply place things silently on the altar-table and be quiet over them long enough to open them and ourselves to the coming God by acknowledging that this and all things and ourselves are from God and unto him. Maybe a little gentle instrumental music.

Once gifts have been taken and the stage is prepared, we are ready to begin the Liturgy of the Eucharist in earnest.

11. The Eucharistic Prayer

Take, bless (give thanks), break, and give. These are the four actions that, as we have said before, shape the Liturgy of the Eucharist. Having taken the bread and wine needed for the celebration and placed them by themselves in the center of our altar-table, we are now ready for the prayer of blessing, the eucharistic prayer, the prayer of thanksgiving.

I remember one noontime, while visiting my sister's family, I was asked to say "the blessing" before the meal. I immediately began, in good Jewish tradition, "Blessed are you, Lord God, King of the Universe. . . ." My sister quizzed me afterwards about why I "blessed" God rather than the meal. I had no immediate answer, although I knew I was doing the truly traditional thing. Jewish meal blessings, indeed any blessing, is ultimately a blessing of God.

Since then I have given the question more thought. Ordinarily, a blessing doesn't so much change the object as it changes its relationship to us and to God. The object is somehow related consciously to God: it comes from him, it is for his service now, and finally returns to him, as all things and persons do. Blessing a meal changes us more than it changes the meal. And how do we make that change? We simply recognize that this thing has come from God and is for him and unto him. We do that by praising and thanking him for his gift. So a prayer of blessing is ultimately a prayer of praise and thanksgiving. All of which means that we are really blessing God, which has as its secondary effect, making us conscious of our own holiness, as his sons and daughters.

At Mass, too, our prayer of blessing is actually a prayer of praise and thanksgiving. Each of the various Eucharistic Prayers (nine in all) available to us today begins by praising and thanking God for his gifts. Usually we begin with thanks for creation, then for the gift of new creation or redemption, maybe making special mention of the particular aspect of the redemptive mystery that we are celebrating on a particular feast day. The congregation joins in the praise, along with all the choirs of angels, in a hymn of praise, which comes to us from the synagogue, "Holy, holy, holy Lord. . . ."

The thanksgiving prayer recalls that the greatest gift, is the gift of God's own Son, given for us in his passion, death and resurrection. The gift of the Son was especially realized (made real) in the gifts of bread and wine at the Last Supper, which we also recall. And so we ask God to be with us now by the coming of the Lord's Spirit in our bread and wine and in our lives. That is, we ask that by the power of the Spirit Jesus might use this bread and wine as the means of making us more fully one in Christ, gaining all the blessings of redemption for which we have been giving thanks and praise.

Having asked this redemption and reconciliation for all the Church, living and dead, we then conclude our prayer, as we began, with a final acclamation of praise: "Through him, with him, and in him in the unity of the Holy Spirit, all glory and honor are yours, now and forever." And everyone joins in, affirming the words of their priest, with the shout of "Amen."

I guess we would have to say that this is the high point of the Mass. Enthusiasm has built right up to this acclamation of praise that sums up the entire stance of a Christian before God, with open arms to receive God's gifts, praising him and professing his faith in this Great Amen.

Of course, it doesn't always come off quite that great. In fact, sometimes it seems like the low point of the celebration, because of the enforced passivity of the congregation and a tendency for the prayers to seem monotonous, colorless and long. Not all of that is the priest's fault, though prayerful and enthusiastic proclamation of the prayer helps some. Dynamic singing of the various acclamations in the prayer helps, too. But certainly the prayers themselves will have to be rewritten in more powerful language.

It is a hard prayer. But effective worship depends on this expression of thanks and praise more than on any other single element.

12. The Communion Rite

The Eucharistic Prayer concluded, we are ready to move on to the final two actions of the Liturgy of the Eucharist: break and give. Maybe we have to reflect for a moment on the symbolism of the Eucharist itself. What are we saying, mostly non-verbally, in this ritual?

The Eucharistic Prayers themselves point out, explicitate, the meaning of celebration. According to them we share in this bread and this wine so that we might "be brought together in unity by the Holy Spirit" or "be filled with his Holy Spirit, and become one body, one spirit in Christ" or, again, so that we might be gathered "into the one body of Christ, a living sacrifice of praise". The word "communion" is a good one for the purpose of the celebration, as long as we understand this word in its full and original meaning: a joining or gathering together. Communion, far from being a rather private moment, is an intensely Communal one. It is a time of heightened awareness of one another and of our bonds to one another in the Christ-Spirit, a spirit of reconciliation and love.

It seems it was refusal to accept one another in the proper spirit and not heretical ideas about bread that led Paul to roundly scold the Corinthians. "Anyone who eats and drinks without recognizing the Body (and these people all around you are the Body of Christ) is eating and drinking his own condemnation."

The principle ways in which the Eucharist symbolizes (and therefore effects, for sacraments are effective signs) this communion with one another in Christ is by our sharing in one bread broken for all and in drinking from the one cup. One loaf, blessed and broken, and one cup, shared by all — these were the symbols Christ used to unite us to one another and himself. If our communities often fail to experience themselves as a community, could it be, at least partly, because we have made this symbol so weak as to be almost unrecognizable? We use hundreds of little, pre-cut wafers; the bread actually broken at a given mass is almost always consumed by the priest alone. Until recently, there was almost no sharing in one cup. The breaking and sharing of one loaf and the sharing in one cup, even if that means pouring from one large vessel into several smaller ones before actually sharing in the cup, is an important way in which we are trying to restore the original meaning of the liturgical signs.

Several small and altogether secondary prayers and gestures accompany this breaking and giving. The Lord's Prayer is the most ancient element. It asks for daily bread in the context of asking for forgiveness, "as we forgive those who trespass against us." The Church sees this prayer as an excellent reflection of the communal nature of the communion rite.

Next, in the Roman Church, we have added the prayer for peace, actually reconciliation might be a more adequate word, because the peace is "the peace which the world cannot give," and the sign of peace. This sign of peace is commonly misunderstood. And this misunderstanding leads some people to suggest moving this gesture to the very beginning of the Mass. But notice that the sign of peace is in no sense a greeting. It is not a time to introduce yourself or to say hello to those around you. That should have been accomplished either before Mass or at the very beginning of Mass. This is a sign that you wish to be joined together in this communion, that you are open to the reconciliation and unification that this sharing will effect if you let it.

After communion, the Mass ends rather simply. A prayer and a blessing send us forth to continue the work begun and symbolized in the Mass just completed.

13. The Silent Times

I want to talk now about the need for silence. I get into this subject knowing that somewhere out there someone is going to be saying, "I told you so." It will be the someone who complained, back when the "new Mass" really was new, that this new Mass didn't allow them time to pray because they were always being talked at, or talking themselves, or being forced to sing.

I am not backing away from my allegiance to the Mass of Paul VI. I want to do this because we live in a busy world. Our lives are strung out and fragmented by all this busy-ness. The Sunday celebration must be a place to gather, to re-collect, those fragments. It will have to be such a place if the Sunday assembly is to be the place that binds us together giving us the courage to go on for another week.

We are hustled and bustled and noised almost to death all week long. We cannot tolerate being rushed into church, raced from penance to praise in a space of time that allows room for neither, fed, and rushed out again. The Eucharist must be a banquet, not a quick lunch in a fast-food establishment.

Far from abandoning my allegiance to the missal of Paul VI and the renovation of the liturgy inaugurated by Vatican II, I want to reinforce the instructions of the Roman Missal, which state quite explicitly, "Silence is an element in celebration which must be given its due place" (General Instruction, No. 23). The instruction goes on to elaborate when that silence ought to take place.

Right at the beginning of the Mass, the instructions call for two distinct moments of silence: Silence at the beginning serves to draw us out of the helter-skelter into the peace. The silence is there to let each person recall his/her need for God before actually calling on him for his merciful assistance and his strength. The second comes in response to the invitation, "Let us pray." In these few moments, we gather our many diverse needs for prayer which the priest "collects" into the Opening Prayer. (Remember when we called it the "collect"?)

Within the Liturgy of the Word, there ought to be moments of silence after each reading, before the response or Alleluia, and also after the homily. In these silences we meditate on what we have heard. Piling the homily on top of the Gospel, on top of the Alleluia, on top of the reading, on top of the psalm, on top of the reading is hardly conducive to hearing, really hearing what God wants to say to us.

In the General Intercession, there is another opportunity for silence. Ideally, there should probably be a couple seconds of this silence after each petition before the invitation, "We pray to the Lord." This would allow and encourage us to reflect on what we have been asked to pray for. Then there can be an extended period of silence after the last petition to add more personal petitions in silence. This pause has to be of sufficient length, since people really do have things to call up for prayer.

The American bishops have made the suggestion that song is not always necessary or desirable at the preparation of the altar table and gifts. This time, too, may be a good time to be quiet. "In fact," they say, "it is good to give the assembly a period of quiet (that is, while the gifts are prepared and placed on the altar) until the introduction to the prayer over the gifts ("Pray, brethren . . .") before demanding, at the preface, their full attention to the Eucharistic Prayer." Those prayers at the preparation of altar table and gifts ("Blessed are you . . ."), then, are best said silently, the bishops are telling us, even when there is no singing going on.

The final call for silence comes after communion. This is a time, we are told, when we "should praise God in our hearts." This period of silence is an exception to the rule, because, in my experience at least, it is generally well observed.

In conclusion, I would just like to repeat the words of the American bishops from the foreword to the missal:

> The proper use of periods of silent prayer and reflection will help render the celebration less mechanical and impersonal and lend a more prayerful spirit to the liturgical rite. Just as there would be no celebration without song, so, too, there should be no celebration without periods for silent prayer and reflection.

PART III

OURSELVES

14. Our Prayer

Some old Roman orator once said that to be a good orator you must first be a good person. The same is true for worship. Being a good man or woman is not enough, for public speaking or for liturgy, but it is fundamental. The reform of the liturgy seems, up until just recently, to have been mostly concerned with moving the furniture, composing new books, using more people, but none of these things will really solve the important problems. The only real answer is spiritual change. It is not the words and furniture that must change now; it is you and I.

We come, therefore, to grips with the real issue: Can I pray? Through careful and patient study, meditation, internalization of texts and gestures, what has until now been mostly words on the pages of the books, conformed to only externally, must change our lives. This will be the most important work of the liturgical reform. Until this has happened, the reform is nothing at all. Until we notice one another, pay attention to one another, love one another, all the words and gestures, all the new furniture and clothing mean little. Until we are truly open to God's action and to hearing his Word, spoken in the many ways of our lives, until we really pray with these new forms, nothing of value has taken place.

Let's admit it. We are all — laypeople, clergy, religious — fairly uncomfortable when talking about prayer. We tend to talk about it only in general, preachy, pious platitudes. Even though the bookstores and publishers' catalogues are bulging with books on prayer, the suspicion remains that there is a conspiracy of silence on the subject. We lack confidence in our ability to pray well, perhaps with good reason, and are therefore embarrassed by being asked to talk about our prayer.

There are formidable obstacles to prayer. They are largely the same obstacles we encounter in all our life. Prayer is ultimately a form of communication. Often the obstacles to free and open communication with God in an individual's life of prayer are the same obstacles that he or she runs up against in attempting free and open communication with husband, wife, neighbor, friend and acquaintance. Even between husband and wife there is often very little real communication about what really matters. Someone who cannot enter into full communication of life with a spouse, may not be able to enter into full communication of life with God either. The problems of prayer must be overcome hand in hand with the overcoming of the problems between ourselves. In the same movement that we learn to open up to one another, we will learn to open up to God and *vice versa*.

Leaders of the liturgical assembly — priests, lay ministers, lectors, ministers of music, etc., should sense that they are leaders of prayer. While priests must certainly learn the "right moves" for celebration, they must also learn how to pray, and not just recite the words of prayer, with their people. You can have the theological training and all the right gestures and speaking skills, but if you lack the desire or ability to pray before and with the assembly, to share your life with them aloud, then you will not be able to celebrate effectively, that is, prayerfully.

To acquire the skills needed for rich prayer you must be willing to confront many questions about your image of God, about your values, about your priorities, about your escapism, about your fears and angers, about your selfishness and about your sin. And you won't be able to do that alone. You must do it with God, of course. But you also must discuss these matters with at least one other or in a small, trusting group.

So the work of the liturgical reform isn't finished in your parish today or tomorrow. And the work of liturgical education and formation is not principally explaining the history of liturgical evolution to people. *The work of prayer is the work of the liturgical reform and it is the work of a lifetime.*

15. Our Community Life

Boredom — flat-out, glassy-eyed boredom, found especially among the young — is the greatest enemy of the Church today. It isn't secularism, communism, protestantism, atheism, materialism, or even the sexual revolution that is doing us in along with our worship. It's boredom.

Once upon a time, I was invited to the celebration of the 50th anniversary of a couple in a parish where I was serving. I didn't know the couple or the family well at all. I suppose I was invited mostly because I was the parish priest. We had nothing in common. We hadn't shared any life together. They had a nice cake, champagne and a band that played great music. There were lots of relatives. I guess they all had a good time. I was mostly bored. Let's face it, though I could put on a good show, I had nothing to celebrate.

Many of our parish celebrations fail because the people there actually have little or nothing to celebrate. Some of that is the problem of prayer. Some of it is the problem of community: they don't know one another nor do they care to. They haven't shared a life together in Christ or otherwise.

I remember being at a workshop on liturgy once where the speaker was asked by a lady in the audience about the boredom in her parish church. The speaker asked about the parish during the week. Well, you can guess what we discovered. This particular parish was dull during the week, too. The two questions are intimately connected. It isn't just a coincidence that a parish that is dull all week is also dull on the weekend.

Furthermore, it is just those who find church the dullest on Sunday mornings who find it the dullest during the week. Think about it. Who likes coming to Mass on Sunday? Usually it is the person who is actively involved in the community's life throughout the week. The little old lady, whose life is so brightened by those Monday night meetings of the whatchamacallit society, where they mostly play cards, is also brightened by Sunday Mass and loves Father's homily, no matter how bad it is. The couple who teaches CCD with enthusiasm each Tuesday evening also enjoys the silence and song together at the Saturday evening Mass. But the teens and young adults, who at least feel that they are offered so little attention during the week, are the ones who stand or sit in the back or in the choir loft and escape at the first chance.

So the task of a worship committee might have to also include a serious look at the life of the community beyond the church walls and outside of the Sunday worship. I doubt that they can address themselves to the tasks that need to be done outside and beyond in a systematic way, but they can't ignore this wider problem. And, at least as individuals, they must attend to this matter.

Anyone who wishes to improve the quality of their Sunday worship beyond a certain point must be willing to become more actively involved in their community, either through organized parish functions, activities and services or through more individualized forms of service in the community.

Father Dennis Kennedy summed it all up for me, "The liturgy expresses who we are as a local church, and if we aren't much, the liturgy expresses that, too."

16. Our Preparation

I am sure that every priest has had the experience of entering the sanctuary full of the spirit of celebration, of greeting the congregation warmly, and of being greeted in return with nothing or with what is worse, the mumbled, mechanical, and the timid, spiritless response. I have more than once celebrated, if that is the right word, with congregations who obviously, if nonverbally, told me that they didn't want to be there. These are the congregations where the hostility is laid on so thick and heavy that you could cut it with a knife. This seems especially true of the last congregation of the weekend. Sunday evening Mass congregations are notoriously unfriendly.

We expect a celebrant to psych himself up for every celebration, even if he celebrates three or more times in a day, to come prepared with appropriate words and with the appropriate spirit, but we make almost no demands on what the congregation should offer. Parishioners can no more come unprepared than the celebrant and other ministers can, not in the Church today.

The first thing each person must do is prepare within himself, before even leaving the house to go to the church. There must be something about the day, Sunday (even if it is Saturday evening), that is special and unique in all the week. I am not saying that we should reinstate the old "blue laws". I think there can be much of value in the increased commercialism and sports activity of Sunday today, looked at and employed in the right spirit. I don't want to go back to the enforced rest of the Puritans or of the Sabbath rest. In all probability, authentic Christian keeping of the Lord's Day doesn't lie in that direction. But the day is different.

I would suggest with others that we think of Sunday as a day of recreation in the fullest sense of the word *"recreation."* It is the "eighth day," the day of the "new creation" by the resurrection of Jesus. So it is a day of "notice the world." It is a day to look around you and enjoy the very good world God has made. For that reflective time, we will have to slow down the pace of the week. Most of us can't notice the world other days, everything goes by so fast.

I am not suggesting spending the day in an explicitly religious manner, like in church on Sunday afternoon for vespers. I think that the Catholic population as a whole, with few exceptions, manages to resist the insistence of pastors in the past who tried to get people back for Sunday vespers or devotions. I am more inclined to think that doing nothing useful and doing that nothing with others, family and friends, in the presence of God's creation, in the Spirit of recreation will turn out to be more truly religious than any vespers service of my experience.

There's more, too, to our preparation. It is more than just a matter of spirit. It is a matter of the "new liturgy" itself. (I wonder when we will stop calling it "new"?) The liturgy today makes greater demands upon the congregation than the previous Sunday worship ever did.

Father Joseph Gelineau has written perceptively on this matter. You see, the "old" assembly was quite tolerant. It was open; that is, it excluded no one. Anyone could "fully" take part, because "fully" taking part meant very little. It was only necessary to be there, physically, for the offertory, the consecration, and the communion (not even receiving communion was necessary, only being there when the priest went to communion). If you were there for that much, you got "full credit." What you actually did while you were there made very little difference. Even though it was encouraged (but only in this century) that you "follow" the Mass, there was no obligation to do so.

Today, to get "full credit," much more is necessary. Even in the merely physical sense, presence is probably necessary from at least five minutes before the celebration and "extra credit" can be obtained by staying for coffee and doughnuts after Mass.

Baptism and some vague religious sense might have once been considered enough. Today you really need a clear and powerful faith for full, active, and conscious participation, demanded by the Vatican Council II. One should really be reasonably well versed in a broad range of scriptural images and allusions. One ought to be thoroughly catechized on the significance of the ritual gestures and aware of their place in the whole of the ritual.

Those with little religious instruction, those on the fringes of the community, those who only show up for the great holidays, or struggling with the mere possibilities of faith will feel themselves virtually excluded from full integration into the Eucharist.

To go to Mass today, you must go prepared.

17. Our Hospitality

Our prayer, our community life, our psychological and spiritual preparation are all elements in getting ready to celebrate effectively. The General Instruction of the Roman Missal only hints at what the next step might be, when it says, "After the people have assembled . . . ." The meaning of that phrase is the next element, one which is frequently ignored.

If you think it just means coming in and sitting down, then you missed it. This step means that a whole bunch of individuals come from doing their own things to doing one thing together; they come from being many to being one.

The congregation is not just a passive audience. Liturgy is not a spectator sport. All this action is not up front. Unfortunately, the word "congregation" conjures up ideas of passivity. They just have to be there physically, to be read to, talked to, to watch, to read along silently and, once in a while, out loud. They "follow the Mass" or "hear the Mass."

The problem is that we have let ourselves be fooled into thinking of other people as a distraction from prayer. Just the opposite is true. People are not a distraction. People are what it's all about, because *this people is the Body of Christ*.

"Among the symbols with which the liturgy deals, none is more important than this assembly of believers . . . The most powerful experience of the sacred is found in the celebration and in the persons celebrating . . . the living sacrifice" (The American Bishops' *Environment and Art in Catholic Worship*).

Romano Guardini, a respected theologian of a couple of decades ago, used to put it this way: "Man is God's way to man." The most effective way to find God at Mass, then, is not "following along," head buried in the missalette. That way you miss the people, focussing on the dead word, instead of the living Word.

We have to pay attention to one another; we have to notice one another. We must allow the feeling of being together to influence us. The Word proclaimed or the prayer prayed by one like yourself who shares his or her faith with you, while you watch and listen to that person's witness of faith, is infinitely more powerful than the words themselves can ever be. Try to hear how these words resonate in the life of the person speaking and ask how they resonate in your own. Sense how these gestures are expressions of faith and prayer, theirs and yours, and blend your words and movements with theirs. You cannot remain emotionally and spiritually isolated. God speaks to us through one another or he does not speak at all.

This role of the community has been described with the word "hospitality." It's a better word than "love" really, which is so loaded with ambiguity. The intimacy implied by that word is simply not possible in congregations the size of ours. Hospitality means, as Fr. Gene Walsh says, "There is room for you right now in my life." We may have never seen one another before; we may never see one another again. I'm not looking to take you home with me. I'm not asking for a permanent relationship or for you to reveal your deepest secrets. But there's room here for you right now.

"Liturgy flourishes in a climate of hospitality," *(Environment and Art in Catholic Worship)* say the American bishops. But what do we do? Often it's like getting on a bus, in an image I acquired from Mr. Gabe Huck. If you have a choice, when you get on a bus, between sitting alone or with someone else, what do you do?

. . . And that's all right. But this isn't a bus. This may

prove to be one of the hardest things for us to learn. But we really have to make room for one another and want to sit together. Congregations who care about one another and pay attention to one another, aware of one another's gifts and needs, always pray well on Sundays, even if the ministers manage their tasks badly.

PART IV

Conditions for Good Worship

18. Ministers of Hospitality

Everyone who takes part in the Eucharistic celebration is called to help create the climate of hospitality which is necessary for worship to flourish. But there is an old principle that if everyone is responsible, then no one is responsible. So if you want your assemblies to be hospitable, then you have to decide whose job being hospitable is.

Traditionally, I guess, it has been the role of the celebrant. He's the host. He welcomes those who come from outside the parish, as well as his parishioners, many of whom he calls by name.

Sometimes, he welcomes with a simple word addressed to all at the beginning of the liturgy. That's good, but not best. Sometimes, he greets individuals as they leave the church on their way home, at the front door or out on the lawn. That's good, too, but it doesn't help assemble the congregation for the celebration.

Really, the only way that the priest can effectively create the climate of hospitality needed for celebration is by greeting people individually at the door before the Mass. That's best, but it means that someone else has to be making sure that everything is set up and ready to go; altar servers ready, special ministers of the Eucharist have reported in, the musicians have coordinated things with the readers, and so forth.

Another thing that helps to gather the assembly and make them aware of one another and of the vital parts that they play in an effective celebration is the warm-up. The leader of song, or a priest, spends five minutes before the celebration begins, briefing the congregation on its role and rehearsing music. This should probably be a standard, every week part of our gathering. It isn't just to learn new music. It is to help foster the atmosphere of hospitality and prepare the congregation to celebrate. No matter who does it, the priest-celebrant should be present for this warm-up. His presence shows that this time is important.

Now, we come to those persons whom we will formally designate "ministers of hospitality," the ushers. The word "usher" is dropping out of the vocabulary of those who are concerned with the quality of our Sunday Masses and the word "collector" is even less helpful. I'm not sure that "ministers of hospitality" will stick as their title, even though it is the term most often used by liturgists today; it's too much of a mouthful.

Ushers have never had that good an image. The very name conjures up pictures of stern, old men, by habit, impersonal and officious. They were more like "bouncers" than "greeters." Many of them probably would have even defined themselves that way. In all fairness, our celebrations were equally cold and forbidding, so they fitted right in. Unfortunately, when the liturgy became, in theory anyway, the joyful song of the redeemed, ushers either resisted the change or were ignored in the process. The time has come to bring them to a new life.

Since their role will be to make people feel comfortable and welcome, to draw them out of themselves into one another, they will have to be warm, outgoing, friendly, sensitive, never phony men and women. They will have to learn to reach out, not just stand by the door and wait. They will have to have a kind word ready and a smile. It might help if they have something in their hands to pass out, like songsheets or even the bulletin. So that they might help set the tone for the day's liturgy, it will help if they are in touch with the overall mood of the Sunday. They would greet people differently in Lent than during the Easter Season.

Once the celebration actually begins, they will have to fade into the woodwork. Even if they also take up the collection, they must do so as unobtrusive servants of the liturgy, never drawing attention to themselves by parading down the center aisle during the preface or dumping coins into baskets when the Holy, holy, holy is being said or sung. The more genuine hospitality they show, the more friendly the coming together will be.

19. Ministering in Many Ways

Greater lay involvement in the life of the church seems to have been the most noticeable outcome of the Second Vatican Council. We have already seen something of the obligations and, therefore, ministry of the whole community. We have spoken too of the ministry of hospitality. Let's take a passing look at the many other ministries.

When we started with all these new roles, our first concern was understandably just to get them filled. The only real requirement in many cases was *good will*. Now, I know, that's important, but it is not enough by itself. We also have to have or be able to acquire certain skills. Volunteerism is dead, at least as the sufficient criterion to fill these roles. Too many teachers don't seem to be able to teach; too many lectors can't read; too many musicians can't play their instruments. Good will is not enough; the proper skills are also important.

The evolution of ministries has gone through stages. For example, first, we had the "Father needs someone to read" stage; second, came the "lay persons have the right, even the duty to serve" stage, now we are in the stage where we must both think of and call these women and men "ministers."

The emphasis needs to shift from the job to the person. Ministry is not something I do. Minister is someone I am. You aren't just filling a function, performing a ministry, you are a minister. Ministry then becomes a way of life. It is the way in which the Spirit has been given in you. It is the way in which you have been reborn in Christ.

The practical results from this new emphasis, though we are not mainly interested in practical results, can be dramatic. Increasing the dignity of the minister, increases proportionately his or her sense of being responsible for that part of the church's life. If you define your life in the Spirit as "lector," as the proclaimer of the Word, then you can never again come unprepared to read your reading. There is also a real carry-over into real, daily life. "Lector" is not just something I do, for a handful of minutes in a church; it is someone I am all the time. I am one who serves the Word with all my life. The cultic performance of my role is simply the culmination of a life of proclamation of the Word.

Each different ministry carries with it a distinct relationship to the church. The ministry you serve in ought to reflect the precise relationship, the precise gift, that you have been given by the Spirit. The determination of which role I will play in the liturgical assembly (and everyone has a distinct role) ought to entail a discernment of the Spirit's movement in my life.

For now, at this particular moment in church history, it may be necessary to reverse this order. We ought to be fostering the development of that spirituality in the ministers we already have, that corresponds to the ministry that they have received.

Lectors will need a spirituality of the Word. This would be a spirituality grounded in a love for and ever deepening understanding of the Scriptures. The prayer life of a lector would probably be centered on reading and meditating on the Scriptures. A lector should be expected to read the Scriptures on a daily basis. Lectors should be the persons in your parish who are the first to want to take part in the Bible study or Bible sharing program that you are beginning, indeed, they should be the ones beginning it. Because, like Ezechiel, they don't merely read the Word but have eaten the scroll, the Word comes forth from them alive and sounds true, that is, it impresses itself on the listeners. The Word has become a part of the reader and has changed his or her life.

A special minister of Holy Communion is a gift-giver. I would think that a gift-giver would be someone who could look people in the eye without embarrassing them or without being embarrassed. A minister of Holy Communion's daily life should show signs of the gathering Spirit, that Spirit that gathers men and women into Christ. A person who is called to this ministry would be the kind of person who reaches out easily to strangers and those in need with a glance or a kind word.

Music is a kind of prayer, even when it is instrumental music. The minister of music develops his or her sensitivity to this artistic way of communing with God. There are snatches of song, antiphons, psalm texts, melodies and hymns that come to mind even without reflection for someone who is spiritually suited to serving in this ministry. In times of sorrow, the Spirit wants to sing, perhaps, a cry for mercy, one of the Lenten antiphons. In times of joy, an acclamation of praise comes to mind and is repeated throughout the day. Song fills the spiritual life of a minister of music and is the most satisfying prayer form.

You see what I mean, I hope. We need to get in touch with the ways in which the Spirit moves in each of us. The ways in which we are the Body of Christ in our daily lives will be the ways we make the Body present in our Sunday assembly. St. Paul's description of the community of Corinth will then begin to become real in our own communities. He says that "each" of the members of that community "contributes a hymn, some instruction, a revelation, an ecstatic utterance, or the interpretation of such an utterance" (I Cor. 1:2; 14:26). All this in accordance with the activity of the Spirit within each individual, in such a way that if any member of the community is missing a given week he or she is missed.

20. Memories of Music

I recall the Holy Week services that I had attended as I was growing up in a small town in Massachusetts. My clearest and earliest recollection of Holy Week was attending one of the big ceremonies and sitting toward the back of the church, where one thing above all impressed me: the music. Some young men were back there in our little choir loft singing all the music for whatever service this was, in Latin, of course. I was very impressed. Was it the quality of their voices, the tone of solemnity and majesty, not without warmth? Who knows? Maybe it was this experience that first directed me toward liturgy and liturgical music.

There are some who maintain all that is now lost. We have now entered into an aesthetic and liturgical wasteland. The great musical tradition of the church is lost, they say. No doubt, many parish liturgies are left with no more than a bare modicum of beauty. This is not only with regard to music. The complaint that they've taken the mystery out of the Mass is not totally unfounded. For some, it seems, relevance and personalism in the reformed liturgy have come to mean sloppy, poorly prepared services, as a counterbalance to the sometimes inhuman precision of the old ways. (Remember when altar boys were drilled like Marines?)

We would be wise not to overstate the case in favor of the old music ways. Let's be honest, that one Holy Week, when I was growing up, was the only time in the years that I lived there that I was impressed. All year long there must have been little or no music, at least none that caught my imagination. During the year most parishes had, at most, one solemn high Mass on the weekend. Most of us attended the other Masses, either because the high Mass was too late in the morning or lasted too long, or were "musicless' and probably even less humanly attractive than what we have today.

Having set the record straight regarding how often, let's look at how well. While I admire the dedication and hard work of the average parish's organist/soloist of the past, the loss of such a one would not always be losing a priceless treasure, artistically speaking. Make no mistake about that last remark. I am merely reflecting on the art, not on the loyalty or even the liturgy. We'll come back to the liturgy question later.

What was sung is worth comment as well: Gregorian chant and Palestrina in many cases; the *Missa de Angelis;* the *Salva Regina,* and a few, rather late almost metrical Latin hymns of dubious quality. Sometimes a Gregorian proper was chanted, but not very often, except at Requiem Masses (which was almost every day, except Sundays).

I am sure that most people believe that that fare is the church's longstanding musical tradition, but it is not. It was only after 1904 (the "revival" under Pope Pius X) that American parishes began to sing such things. Except in France, Belgium, and Switzerland, few Catholics would have ever heard a single piece of real Gregorian chant before then. There was no authentic edition of Gregorian chant until after 1905, and it was not listed as a category of church music officially until 1958!

Palestrina and all that classical polyphony only really caught on in the late 17th and 18th centuries. To act as though such a repertoire is the church's heritage from Gregory the Great (died A.D. 604) is simplistic at best.

Then there is intelligibility. Rarely could you make out the words even if you had understood them, since they were in Latin and even if you understood Latin, the texts didn't always make a great deal of sense for they assumed the congregation had a great knowledge of the psalms. What congregation, hearing the psalm text on the Feast of Ephiphany, *"Deus, judicium tuum regi da, et justitiam tuam filio regis,"* would realize that this text was being used because ten verses further into the psalm (which were not going to be sung) there were some very clear references to the Epiphany story?

No, the music of the past was not the golden age and today's music cannot be written off as a wasteland. It isn't that simple. We need music that fills its ministerial function.

21. Ministry of Music

Several years ago, when I was still going to school, I had the opportunity to hear the Vienna Choir Boys sing at a Sunday liturgy. The music was fantastically beautiful, as I had expected. But I went away very angry. For, although this was supposed to be a Mass, in fact, the congregation had been allowed no role at all. There had been no congregational singing, no chance for us even to respond in the spoken word, and, to top it off, we hadn't even been given a chance to receive Communion. We had attended a concert. The Eucharist was little more than a backdrop, the staging for the choir boys.

Probably all of us, at one time or another, have found ourselves in a similar — though perhaps not quite so extreme — situation. It isn't always a big choir that is the offender: It can be a small folk group, just as easily, or even a soloist (even the celebrant), using a captive audience to display his marvelous talents.

Beautiful sounds are important for good celebration. Music provides a dimension, when well done, that cannot be provided in any other way. It creates an aura of joy and enthusiasm, of wonder and solemnity, of meaning and feeling which words alone could never yield. Letting go of your cold logic, you can be caught up in the beautiful noise and discover the God within and behind all beauty. The cheap, trite, and tawdry sounds coming from some of our solemn assemblies, by contrast, can never hope to evoke God.

Do not, however, confuse musical style with musical

value. We need music of value, that is artistically sound. I would hope that people of artistic and musical competence would be allowed to make this judgment of what is or is not good music. Even among musicians, however, there are those who are unaware of the distinction between style and value. There is good, contemporary music in the folk idiom and there is bad, contemporary music in the same idiom. There is also good music from the 18th century and there is bad music from the same period. Not all classical-style music is good, not all contemporary-style music is bad. We must have a broad enough vision to discover music of value in any style and no style is necessarily excluded from the liturgical assembly.

Of course, not all music of value is suitable for liturgy as we saw with the Vienna Choir Boys. The goal of music in celebration, after all, is not obtaining the perfect musical rendition. The goal is drawing humankind into the mystery. The goal is full, conscious, and active participation. The musical judgment is basic, but it is by no means the only or final judgment to be made. A pastoral judgment must also be made. We strive for musical perfection but we keep in mind the words of St. Augustine: "Do not allow yourselves to be offended by the imperfect while you strive for the perfect." And, as Father Lucien Deiss points out in his book, *Spirit and Song in the Liturgy*, "The sound of people singing has a special beauty all its own."

Does this particular piece of music, in this particular congregation, at this particular time, in this cultural milieu help these people express and experience their faith and the faith of the church? This is the pastoral judgment that no musician, as such, is capable of making. To answer this question, we must consider the musical capabilities of each individual congregation both in performing and in listening to good music. We must consider such diverse and ever-changing considerations as time of day (the 7 a.m. Mass on a weekday looks very little like the 11 a.m. Mass on Sunday), the time of year, the age, and background of the congregation, and any number of other intangibles.

The interplay of these two judgments, musical and pastoral, speaks again to us of the need for a team approach to planning liturgy, since only very rarely will one person be proficient in making both of these judgments. There is still another judgment that must be made on any piece of liturgical music: the liturgical judgment.

22. The Rhythm of Worship

I would like to simply list the various parts of the Mass that either are or might be sung and evaluate liturgically the importance of singing at such a time. The criteria for evaluation is now liturgical. This is the third judgment one makes in choosing music for liturgy. The other two already mentioned are the aesthetic and the pastoral.

Entrance Procession — Its purpose is to gather the community into one. It should therefore ordinarily be sung by all the congregation.

Lord, have mercy — A secondary rite which should be emphasized only rarely (Lent?). A choir could help the congregation.

Glory to God — Its length and lack of metrical form make it very hard to sing effectively. To sing it puts emphasis on the mere introduction to the liturgy itself. This could be sung only rarely with or without the congregation wholly involved.

The Responsorial Psalm — Ordinarily it should be sung. Psalms are songs and are almost meaningless when simply read. It is an important part of the Liturgy of the Word.

The Alleluia — Should absolutely never be recited.

Omit it if you are not going to sing it. Sing it often. It announces the Gospel which is the center of the Liturgy of the Word.

The Creed — It is preferable that this be spoken. It should never be sung by the choir alone.

Offertory Procession — Neither always necessary or desirable. Good place for a choir or instrumental music.

Preface and Eucharistic Prayer — Music has been included in the Sacramentary for all the prefaces and all the Eucharistic Prayers (in the appendix). It would be wonderful if we could give the emphasis due this central moment in the Mass.

Holy, holy, holy — We join the choirs of angels and archangels and we sing. Every Preface implies that this is inappropriate to simply recite. Never by choir alone.

Memorial Acclamation — A very important moment heightened by song. Not quite as important as the holy, holy, holy, but almost.

The Doxology and Great Amen — Sung, of course. To be more effective it may be repeated or augmented. The choir may add parts but should never sing it alone.

The Our Father and its doxology — This is the central moment of the communion rite in many ways and could well be sung, though it is not essential.

Lamb of God — Merely to accompany the breaking of the bread, a secondary rite that could be sung by the whole congregation or by the choir or by any combination of these two. It is not terribly effective when read, but given the present state of the breaking rite it is not terribly important anyway. As we begin using real bread which must be broken and wine which must be poured, singing will help here.

Communion Procession — Really ought to have singing with it. Antiphonal singing of a short and simple response with choir or cantor singing verses seems to work well.

After Communion — Sometimes, song here can be very effective to create an atmosphere of communal prayer. If there has been a song sung by all during communion, this will not be as valuable without a silent pause first. The choir and/or cantor can do a lot at this point.

Recessional — Although we think of it as almost mandatory, it is not. In fact, I wonder about saying, "Go in peace", but then asking the congregation to stick around for three verses of whatever. A choir or instrumental piece could well accompany the ministers as they depart. At any rate, there is a lot of room for freedom here.

23. Environment and Worship

Once upon a time, there was a committee that was functioning very badly. Things were going so inefficiently, as a matter of fact, that there were many, many complaints about the inadequacy of the chairman and a replacement was about to be requested. One of the people associated with the committee happened to be an architect, a very gifted one at that. He had reason to believe that the chairman was not the problem, but the meeting room was. He set about changing the environment for the meeting, changing the furniture around, changing the lighting, some of the colors and textures, and so forth. Lo and behold, as if by magic, the meetings became more effective. Space is one of the major factors in good communication, though we rarely give it the attention that it deserves.

The late Winston Churchill once observed, "We shape our buildings and they shape us." He was concerned that the restoration of the House of Commons after World War II would seriously alter the patterns of government.

Is it any wonder that we are finding it difficult to foster a "Vatican II" worshiping Church, when we are, by and large, trying to do it in an essentially, still "Vatican I" space? You may say that we have renovated our churches, but I suspect that we have done very little adequate renovation.

Let me tell you another story. A doctor noticed in a hospital in Canada that some spaces kept people apart and other spaces brought people together. Railway or airport waiting rooms kept them apart, for example. Cocktail lounges and sidewalk cafes brought them together. This doctor also noticed that after visiting hours, the staff went around and lined up the chairs in stiff, military rows undoing the little circles and clusters they formed when people used them to be with one another. He also noticed that the longer the patients stayed in the wards, the more they become like the furniture: stiff, silent, glued to the walls and floors, and slightly depressed.

It is true in worship as well. Long before the first gesture is made or the first word spoken, gestures and words which we like to think will form a Christian community, the group is already formed by the space it is in.

Our theology tells us that the congregation assembled is the first and most important symbol of the Eucharist, as we discussed earlier, but our churches often tell us something else. Our theology tells us that the congregation is not an audience, but an active participant, indeed, each individual in his or her individuality is important. Our church architecture sometimes says something else.

This is not the time or place to examine all the possibilities and options. It is only the time to ask that you examine the shapes, colors, textures, materials, heights and depths that shape your liturgy even more than your theology does. What is the personality of the space in which you pray together?

Is the space you worship in "sociopetal" or "sociofugal"? That is, does it encourage interpersonal activity or does it tend to keep people apart? Most pre-Vatican II churches were purposely, if unreflectively, built in a way that left individuals alone with God rather than together with him.

Is the space in which you worship dynamic or static? Are people in nailed down, regimented rows of pews in a passive rectangular arrangement, where they only see the backs of heads? Tell people in that situation to be active in the liturgy and they experience the contradiction.

Do you want to foster a God-in-people attitude or a God-localized-in-the-sanctuary attitude? Or somehow both? Is the presence of God and the communication of the presence the same in the liturgy of the Word as in the liturgy of the Eucharist?

Are the liturgy of the Word and the liturgy of the Eucharist separate but equal? Do they demand different kinds of space? Why do the guidelines say that the altar-table is to be placed "in the midst of the people"?

Then there are an equal number of questions about color. Different colors communicate and create different kinds of space. Height, length, density, width all communicate and create a concept of worship.

We are largely unable to celebrate a post-Vatican II liturgy in a Tridentine space. Until we have new space for our worship, our congregations will resist doing what we are asking of them.

24. Our Food for Worship

We all want to make our Sunday celebrations clear and powerful expressions of our faith. We all want to enliven and enrich our Sunday gatherings. Sometimes we even engage ourselves in extensive and expensive efforts to attain this end. Unfortunately, our efforts are sometimes less effective than they might be. The reason for this is that we often only concern ourselves with the secondary symbols of our liturgy and neglect the primary symbols, where our impact could be greater with less effort.

The primary symbols of our worship are elements like the people assembled, the bread and the wine. Elements like banners, flowers, music, vestments, the furniture, what the special ministers of Holy Communion wear, the size, shape and sex of altar servers are at best secondary elements. We have already spoken about hospitality. Hospitality is the care we take with that primary symbol — the assembly. After the assembly, perhaps the most important symbols are the bread and the wine in which we all share to become one in Christ.

To return to the church's tradition of allowing every member of the assembly to receive Communion under both forms, bread and wine, is one step in the direction of caring for primary symbols. Sharing in the one cup in fulfillment of the Lord's command, "Take this, all of you, and drink from it", restores what may not be a legally necessary element, but it is an important element ritually and symbolically. I feel we are still missing the boat, though, by neglecting in most cases the important symbol of the breaking and sharing one loaf of bread.

In most churches the bread fails to even vaguely resemble bread and is rarely broken so that even a few of the faithful can share in it. This falls far short of the standards set for bread in the official books and guidelines, such as the *General Instruction of the Roman Missal* and the *Third Instruction on the Correct Implementation of the Constitution on the Sacred Liturgy.*

Here are those standards:

1) the bread should look like real food
2) it should be made from wheat flour
3) it should be unleavened, according to the Latin tradition
4) it should be able to be broken and shared by at least some of the faithful
5) the faithful should ordinarily receive from bread consecrated at that same Mass
6) the integrity of the sign demands more attention to the color, taste, and texture of the bread than to its shape.

The wafers we use in most churches on most Sundays fail to meet more than half of these requirements.

A brief review of the history of bread reveals how this situation has come about. Though Jesus almost certainly used unleavened bread for the Last Supper, the early Church felt no need to use only unleavened bread for the Eucharist. They simply used whatever bread was available. Through the centuries they used bread supplied by parishioners, their ordinary supply of bread for their own tables. One of the more popular kinds was a twisted braid woven into the shape of a crown. There were also breads scored on top before baking, for ease of breaking and for decorative purposes.

In the Latin Rite, in the ninth century, some local churches began insisting on the use of unleavened bread only. They liked the idea that this probably conformed more to what Jesus had done. They also wanted to remove the bread as far as possible from the sphere of the "ordinary." This was all happening during the time when fewer and fewer people were receiving the Eucharist. Receiving under both species was eliminated along with receiving in the hand. Anyway, it was hardly the Golden Age of Eucharistic devotion. Rome was late, as usual, in adopting the new custom of using only unleavened bread, which was very much unlike real food. Rome came to this practice only in the eleventh century.

Now that we hare restored our emphasis on frequent reception of the Eucharist, receiving under both species, receiving in the hand, and so many other more traditional practices, it seems to be time to do something about the poor quality of our bread.

There are literally hundreds of bread recipes all over the country for use at Mass. Some are better than others. Some clearly fail to meet the requirements. Some seem to succeed rather well. There are still questions we need to address to clarify what we want to use in our country today. One of these questions is, "What constitutes unleavened bread?" The Jews insist on a "poor bread," made of only flour and water, for the Passover meal. We know, however, of other "richer" breads containing such things as sugar, honey, milk, oil, and eggs. Another important question is whether any "poor bread" can meet the standards set for Eucharistic bread, especially the requirement that it appear as real food to Americans?

Whatever we finally decide as a Church, this attention to primary symbols will not go unrewarded. It will make even clearer the meaning of the Eucharistic banquet.

Conclusion: The Future

The public worship of the Church has evolved for centuries. The Church, after all, is a living organism. It's growth, like yours and mine, has been slow, almost imperceptible, but real nonetheless. If you asked someone in the third century if the liturgy were changing, you'd have been told, probably, that it was not. But look at the liturgy of the second century and the liturgy of the fourth and you know that it was changing all the time. One age would feel the need to highlight one aspect of prayer. Another would want to highlight another. One century would emphasize the elements of praise and thanksgiving in the Eucharist. The next would want to emphasize the elements of forgiveness and reconciliation. One period spawned new feasts. Another pruned them back. New music and new art forms were continuously being tried.

Of course, what happened was that everything seemingly came to a grinding halt. Liturgy was put in a strait jacket. Bound up like that, the pressures built up tremendously. Then, suddenly, or so it seemed, the dam burst. That led to a huge explosion. Some of the energy was destructive and some creative. What is needed now is time. The natural forces of evolution will, with time give ever more adequate form to our public prayer forms. If not bound up again by well-meaning liturgists, liturgy will harmonize more and more with Christians' lives as they are lived in the future.

The cast has been taken off. Now we will need a lot of therapy and exercise and trial and error (don't be afraid to make mistakes) before we have our full strength back.

As the years go on, we will find that even more changes are needed. The liturgical reform is not over. The Church is always reforming itself. Maybe we'll find ways to improve on the introductory rites of the Mass. Maybe we can simplify the Communion rites. Maybe we will find that the preparation of the altar and gifts is not expressing exactly what our theology is saying that this rite ought to say. Maybe we can find Eucharistic prayers of more linguistic power. I don't even want to guess what all the changes will be. But if you think the Mass has changed a great deal in the last decade, stick around with me and see what happens in the next 20 years or so!

If you have the sensitivity to our brothers and sisters' needs and a firm grasp of tradition, rightly understood, the future evolution will be painless. It will not seem like the "violent" change of the last decade.

Moving into the future, I'll be keeping in mind words of Father Godfrey Deikmann, O.S.B., one of the brightest lights of the last half century of worship in America. Father tells the following story about something that happened to him in Rome during the Vatican Council II, where he was an official consultant on liturgy. Let me simply quote the story from *Worship* (vol. 51, number 4):

> The importance of lived experience of the liturgy was brought home to us especially one evening during the Council by the late Bishop Spuelbeck from Meissen, East Germany. He asked that his remarks be off the record, for if they became public, he would not be allowed back into East Germany. He reminded us that the communists have their own pseudoliturgies, and that all the normal Catholic societies had been abolished. The only thing that the Catholics have is the Sunday Mass. He begged us to be as radical as we could possibly be about the revision of the rites, especially of the Mass, so that it could again become an experience of common identity, of shared faith and of love to his people. For it is

Conclusion: The Future 87

the one thing that holds them together, to cling to, to which they come Sunday after Sunday to draw new hope. His talk to us was one of the inspirational moments that profoundly influenced the work of the preparatory commission.

Testimonies

Only God knows how many lives have been touched by Linda's cards/devotionals! They go with me everywhere I go—restaurants, ball games, soccer games, hospitals, doctor appointments, nursing homes, hair salons, motels in various states (approximately 10), even a yard sale or two! Without fail, God puts people in my path who need encouragement, or know someone who does, because of cancer or some other serious illness. I don't know who is more blessed, the people receiving her messages, or me.

But I think what touches me the most is when God sends nurses my way who work in an oncology office or on the oncology floor of a hospital, and I am able to give them devotionals to pass out to patients, because that was Linda's heart. She liked to deliver cards and baskets of encouragement and sit with people while they were getting their treatments. She truly lived out the Scripture verses in 1 Corinthians 1:3-4 which say, "The God of all comfort, . . . comforts us in all our troubles, so that we can comfort those in any trouble with the comfort we ourselves have received from God."

It is truly a privilege to be even a small part of this ministry that is reflecting God's light and touching lives everywhere it goes! I can't wait to see what God has planned for it next.

To Him be the glory forever and ever. In Jesus' name and for His fame. Amen!!!

~ Julie Perry,
Reflecting Light Ministry Supporter

I had the privilege of caring for Linda on her cancer journey. From that journey sprang forth an outreach ministry focused on messages aimed to provide strength and comfort to others on that same journey. Linda had a deep insight into what others were going through. This was reflected in her inspirational messages, which were anticipated and enjoyed by other patients, families, friends, and staff members. She truly had an exceptional gift which she gladly shared with many.

~ Denise Olthaus, RN
The Christ Hospital Physicians Hematology, Oncology

Testimonies

Thank you, Linda, for all the encouragement you sent me during my cancer battle. I have shown many of your cards/devotionals to others making this journey, and I will be passing your name on to others who need encouragement and knowledge that God is with us as we battle cancer. I praise God that He allowed you to do this wonderful work on His behalf.

~ Jan Watsell, Cancer Pilgrim

Each of Linda's devotionals is a written prayer of hope and encouragement for people desperate for hope and encouragement. As a member of Linda's Bible study group we helped her assemble the devotionals as individual cards; and we, with Linda, prayed over them. We prayed that each card recipient would find peace and clarity. We also prayed that God would reveal the plans that he had for them and their families. I have seen the fruit of those prayers in the testimonies of many pilgrim readers.

~ Richard Sunberg
Reflecting Light Ministry Supporter

In *It's Cancer!*, Linda's beautifully written devotions reassure fellow travelers through serious illness that the peace and strength she found in her friendship and walk with Jesus will help them as well. This book is perfect if you are facing an illness of any kind and would be a thoughtful gift for a loved one or friend.

~ Donna J. Shepherd, Author

*A 52-week devotional
from one pilgrim's personal
encounters with God*

It's CANCER!

Linda Benz Kovarik

It's Cancer
A 52-week devotional from one pilgrim's personal encounters with God

Copyright © 2015 by Joe Kovarik

Print ISBN 13: 978-0-9908628-0-2
eBook ISBN 13: 978-0-9908628-1-9

ORDERING INFORMATION
Joe Kovarik, Administrator
Reflecting Light Ministry, LLC
PO Box 277 • Vandergrift, PA 15690
Office: 724-571-7151 • Fax: 866-924-1602
reflectinglight@live.com
www.reflectinglightministry.com

ALL RIGHTS RESERVED. No part of this publication may be reproduced, distributed, or transmitted in any form or by any means, including photocopying, recording, or other electronic or mechanical methods, without the prior written permission of the publisher, except in the case of brief quotations embodied in critical reviews and certain other noncommercial uses permitted by copyright law. For permission requests, write to the publisher, addressed "Attention: Permissions," at the address above.

Scriptures marked AMP are taken from Amplified Bible Copyright © 1954, 1958, 1962, 1964, 1965, 1987 by The Lockman Foundation

Scriptures marked ESV are taken from The ESV® Bible (The Holy Bible, English Standard Version®) copyright © 2001 by Crossway.

Scriptures taken from the Holy Bible, New International Version®, NIV®. Copyright © 1973, 1978, 1984, 2011 by Biblica, Inc.™ Used by permission of Zondervan. All rights reserved worldwide. www.zondervan.com The "NIV" and "New International Version" are trademarks registered in the United States Patent and Trademark Office by Biblica, Inc.™

Scriptures marked NLT are taken from The Open Bible, New Living Translation, Copyright © 1998 by Thomas Nelson, Inc.

Scriptures marked KJV are taken from The King James Version of The Holy Bible, which is in the public domain.

Scriptures marked NKJV are taken from The Personal Study Bible, New King James Version, Copyright © 1990, 1995, by Thomas Nelson, Inc.

Scriptures marked WEB are taken from The World English Bible, a 1997 revision of the American Standard Version of the Holy Bible, first published in 1901. It is in the Public Domain.

Scriptures marked MEV are taken from The Holy Bible, Modern English Version. Copyright © 2014 by Military Bible Association. Published and distributed by Charisma House.

*To all those who are seeking
hope, meaning, and encouragement
on their own pilgrimage with cancer.*

TABLE OF CONTENTS

Dedication v
The Pilgrimage 1

TRANSFORMING MY DARKNESS INTO HIS LIGHT 3
   1. All Things Become New 4
   2. Light Up Your World 6
   3. Love My Enemies? 8
   4. Twinkle, Twinkle Little Star 12
   5. Hold On! 14
   6. Sparkles for Your Day 16

HE LOVES ME 19
   7. You're the Apple of My Eye 20
   8. He Loves Me, He Loves Me Not 22
   9. My Heart Is How Big? 24
  10. What a Sky 28
  11. I Am Wonderfully Made 30
  12. A Warm Smile from God's Love 32
  13. Sing! 34

HIS PROMISES ARE FOR ME FOREVER 37
  14. Take Me Out to the Ballgame 38
  15. When It Rains, It Pours and Pours and Pours 40
  16. Let Go, Let God 43
  17. Powerful! Alive! 46

I WILL FEAR NOT, BUT TRUST 47
  18. I Am 50
  19. It's Cool 54
  20. Save Me, Lord! 56
  21. Trouble Lurking About 60
  22. I'm Gonna Getcha 62

Table of Contents

PUTTING HIS GLADNESS IN MY HEART 65

23. It's So Unfair! 66
24. If Only 68
25. Putting Gladness in My Heart 70
26. Flowers are Smiles from God 72

DAILY VICTORY GOD'S WAY 75

27. Need a Little Sunshine? 76
28. Beeing a Busy Bee 78
29. This Way? Or That Way? 80
30. Thou Shalt Be a Stickler 82
31. May All Your Wishes Come True 84
32. Feeling Weary? 86

LIVING CONFIDENTLY IN HIS STRENGTH 89

33. He's Got the Whole World in His Hands 90
34. Good Night Sleep Tight 92
35. Looking Good 94
36. Come and See 96
37. Just Hanging Around 98
38. Yum! 100

TRUE FRIENDS ARE FOREVER 103

39. Feeling Alone? 104
40. Heaven Is Watching Over You 106
41. Friends Share the Joy and Divide the Sorrow 108
42. I'm Here for You! 110

KEEP FAITH ALIVE 113

43. The Power of Prayer in Times of Uncertainty 114
44. Treasures of the Snow 118
45. What Did I Forget to Remember? 120
46. Liberty 122
47. Keep the Faith 124

Table of Contents

Hugs & Hope for the Holy Holidays...127
 48. May Christmas Hug Your Heart 128
 49. The Power of the Resurrection 130
 50. Tale of Three Trees.. 132

A Time to Give Thanks & Focus on a New Year.......................135
 51. It's Thanksgiving 136
 52. It's a New Year 140

Epilogue... 143
Acknowledgments 145
Scripture Notes... 146
My Reflections 149

The Pilgrimage

The Lord my God lightens my darkness.
~ Psalm 18:28

I am an experienced pilgrim of illness. As a child, I endured the path of several surgeries on my left arm due to a bone infection, which resulted in limited use of my hand. As a young adult, I followed the path again when in my late twenties, I was treated twice for Hodgkin's Lymphoma. As an adult, I embarked on a dark, looming path when in 1998 I was diagnosed with breast cancer. As a couple, my husband Joe and I understand the shock of the diagnosis of cancer and the stress of living with chronic illness. We have both been pilgrims on a life-altering journey.

The diagnosis of a serious illness wreaks havoc with our spirits, emotions, and bodies. Day by day, step by step, we travel this new road trying to be brave and strong while searching for understanding, searching for hope, searching for comfort.

My cancer is in remission as I write this, but I continue on the path challenged by new ailments. Yet, the road doesn't seem so dark and frightening now. We are learning each day to trust God who faithfully strengthens us and gives us hope and comfort on each step of the pilgrimage.

My husband and I started Reflecting Light Ministry to share the source of comfort and strength with others who are on their own pilgrimage with a serious illness. This source gave us light through the dark days of my cancer and gives the same light every day to all who seek it.

My Pilgrimage Devotional

This pilgrimage devotional includes one message for every week of the year. They are arranged by life topics so that on any day or week, you can turn to the section that will speak most directly to your current emotional, spiritual, or physical need. At various points there are lined pages for you to stop and reflect on how God is encountering you on your daily pilgrimage. You may want to write more in your own journal, or you may not have anything to write. Both are okay.

As you read these devotionals, may they help to brighten your day, give you a laugh, encourage you on your journey with cancer, and let you know that you are not alone.

Dear Lord,

I now have developed a disease which I have often feared. I am afraid. I am lonely. Questions seem to crowd my mind: Will I be cured? Will there be pain? How long will I live? How will my family handle this? I ask with all my heart that I be healed. But, if my healing is not in Your great plan, I trust You to be with me through it all. I trust You to give me peace, to let me live with hope, to relieve any pain, and to let me know Your presence. I trust You to bring my loved ones close to me during this illness, that we might support each other, and that Your great hands might support us all.

O Lord, even as I suffer from my illness, I believe in Your might. Even as I am besieged by armies of pain, I seek refuge in You. Help me to feel Your presence even more firmly in my life. Give me courage to face anything, to endure everything with You by my side, that I may bless Your Holy Name.

Amen.

~ Anonymous prayer by a cancer patient

Transforming My Darkness
INTO HIS LIGHT

1
ALL THINGS BECOME NEW
God's Encouraging Metamorphosis

*Therefore, if anyone is in Christ, he is a new creation;
old things have passed away;
behold, all things have become new.*
~ 2 Corinthians 5:17

Do you remember the first time you found a mysterious-looking cocoon on a branch? Curiosity grew as you watched daily with anticipation, hoping to witness the emergence of a new creation. The miraculous metamorphosis of a wiggly worm into a beautiful butterfly captures the imagination of young and old.

In its dark cocoon the worm submits to the supernatural process changing it into a new butterfly. The metamorphosis takes time, and breaking free from its old cocoon is hard and laborious. But oh, what a marvelous, miraculous, beautiful new creation emerges into the light and flies away!

Metamorphosis means a change of physical form, structure, or substance especially by supernatural means, or a striking alteration in appearance, character, or circumstances.

Changes occur continually in our lives, but not as dramatically as the metamorphosis that takes place when we are diagnosed with cancer. We become surrounded by a dark cocoon of stressful change, invoking a striking alteration of our physical appearance, our personal character, and our lifestyle circumstances.

Do you feel like you are confined in a cocoon by cancer as you strive to cope with the changes that have transformed your life? Remember the metamorphosis of the worm, and know that God is supernaturally working in your circumstances. Trust His transforming love to give you wings of hope, lifting you up for new vision and purpose beyond cancer. The process may feel hard and laborious, but through the love of Christ, you can emerge from your cocoon of cancer into His light as a marvelous, miraculous, beautiful new creation!

Dear God,

Each day when I wake up and realize I am still in this cocoon with cancer, help me to remember Your metamorphosis process—You are here with me working to transform me into a miraculous new creation. Thank You for the hope You give me for the time I will break free from this cocoon and fly away with You!

In Jesus' name I pray, amen.

---

*May you fly freely in His divine light,
a new creation remade with His purpose and love.*

2

LIGHT UP YOUR WORLD

The Power of Light in Times of Darkness

> Jesus said, "I am the light of the world."
> ~ John 8:12

"I know it must be close. It shouldn't be difficult to see," my husband and I commented to each other as we drove along the shore of Lake Erie looking for Marblehead Lighthouse. We expected to see a large structure boldly rising above the surrounding rooftops. After driving up and down the road, we finally saw a small sign directing us where to turn. There on the rocky point of Sandusky Bay stood the 65-foot white conical stone tower, looking like a proud sentinel watching over the boats passing by on Lake Erie, as it had been doing for the past 180 years. Later that evening we looked back over the bay and marveled how the lighthouse, which we did not see easily during the light of day, was now so obviously visible.

While the lighthouse remained ever watchful during the light of day, the full brightness and strength of its light beamed forth as darkness enveloped Lake Erie—a comfort to passing mariners. Looking toward the light, they could securely maneuver their boats through the waters avoiding the rocky shoreline of the bay.

The Lord Jesus is ever watchful during the daylight of your daily routines, although you may not always be aware of Him.

Transforming My Darkness into His Light

When the darkness of a diagnosis of cancer closes in around you, be assured the strength of His light will shine brightly. Look toward the light of Jesus with prayer and faith. You will find comfort and hope as He helps you securely maneuver through the challenging times of your journey with cancer. He is the light of your world.

Lord Jesus,

Sometimes the darkness of this cancer overwhelms me, and I don't know how I will make it through. Help me see Your light and feel the strength of Your love, hope, and comfort beaming forth into my heart today.

In Your name I pray, amen.

May Jesus' "lighthouse" guide you securely through your journey with cancer.

3

LOVE MY ENEMIES?

The Power of Faith in Times of Weakness

> *But I say to you, love your enemies.*
> *~ Matthew 5:44*

This is a tough teaching—love your enemies. Jesus was not giving a motivational speech to the crowd on how to improve relationships and live in peace. He was giving a divine command, a command He lived out through the grueling crucifixion when He prayed as He hung on the cross, *"Father, forgive them."*[1]

Jesus' command is difficult enough to live out with the people around us, but how do you apply it to an enemy like cancer or serious illness? There are many interpretations of Jesus' teaching on how it applies to life today, and there are varying viewpoints on how to face a serious illness like cancer. For some it is not a battle with an enemy that has attacked their bodies, but it is something to be embraced and lived with while working with their bodies to overcome the illness. Others celebrate the experience because the illness motivated them to make positive life changes. "This was the best thing that ever happened to me."

Everyone must choose their own path along the journey with an illness. I have not come to the point in my journey of embracing or celebrating my illnesses. Rather, I feel that I am still in a battle with enemies, namely cancer and now rheumatoid arthritis.

I live with the knowledge that because I have battled cancer three times, I am considered at high risk of recurrence. I live daily with the effects of rheumatoid arthritis attacking my joints and draining my strength and energy. So how do I fulfill Jesus' command to love my enemies? How do I love the companions of these enemies—fear, anxiety, depression, despair, anger, worry—that have tried to attack me mentally and emotionally?

The Apostle Paul endured many hardships and attacks from his enemies who wanted to silence him during his ministry years. He was shipwrecked, beaten, imprisoned, and struggled with discouragement at times. Through all of this he also lived with a chronic affliction that weakened him physically. Yet, he declared, *"When I am weak, then I am strong."*[2] What was his source of strength? Paul said that through all his trials he had learned, *"I can do all things through Christ who strengthens me."*[3]

I have learned when I strive to go forward on my own strength, that although I may experience small successes along the way, I will ultimately fail miserably. Now when I awake in the morning and drag out of bed, loosening up my swollen stiff achy joints, I am reminded how much I need my source of strength. Some days are better than others, but each twinge of a joint during the day is a reminder to stay focused on Christ.

Yes, I can love my enemies, cancer, and rheumatoid arthritis (RA), because they compel me to turn to Christ, my Savior. Through His strength, I can live a relatively normal life with few restrictions and minimal medication for RA. Through His strength I am assured that I will ultimately succeed victoriously over my illnesses.

I pray whatever your viewpoint is toward your diagnosis of cancer, whether you embrace it, celebrate it, or battle it, that you know Jesus Christ as your source of strength. Through His strength and love you can be certain of ultimate victorious success!

Dear Jesus,

When I am feeling weak, let me realize Your strength enables me to "do all things" through this journey with cancer. Thank You for being with me.

In Your name I pray, amen.

My Reflections

Transforming My Darkness into His Light

4

Twinkle, Twinkle Little Star

Lift up your eyes and look to the heavens:
Who created all these?
He who brings out the starry host one by one,
and calls them each by name.
Because of his great power and mighty strength,
not one of them is missing.

~ Isaiah 40:26

"Twinkle, twinkle little star, how I wonder what you are." Did you sing that as you gazed up at the heavens on a clear night when you were a child? Or looked up with expectancy to the brightest star you saw and wished, "Star light, star bright, first star I see tonight, I wish I may, I wish I might have this wish I wish tonight"? Or simply laid back in awe and wonder at the vastness of millions of stars and planets? Did it make you pause and ponder over the Creator of the majesty of the night sky? Did you question, "If God is so powerful and great to place each star in place, will He reach down and involve Himself in my life?"

Have you questioned His involvement since you were diagnosed with cancer? I did. I doubted and questioned when I received my third diagnosis of cancer. I remember going out in my backyard looking up to the night sky and asking God, "Where are You? I want to believe, but You seem so far away. I wish this cancer would go away."

Transforming My Darkness into His Light

The Israelites were in a situation they wished would go away. They were in the middle of a long-term trial faced with threats from their enemy and the certainty of years of captivity. They questioned God's willingness to help them. They questioned God's presence in their lives.

God heard them and gave a message of assurance for the prophet Isaiah to deliver to His people who were doubting Him. Isaiah encouraged them to look up to the stars and remember the greatness of God's might and power. God calls each star by name and places them in their proper course so not one fails. The Israelites could find assurance that He also knew each of His children by name and that the strong power of His presence was with them through the course of their uncertain trials.

As captives of cancer we experience many doubts—even doubts about God. Doubts can cause us to feel helpless and hopeless. Doubts can disrupt our healing process. When these doubts plague us and we question God, we can look up to the stars, and instead of wishing, we can find assurance that He hears us. We find assurance in the One "who created all these" in His might and power. Most of all, we find assurance that He calls each of us by name, and His faithful presence is with us throughout the course of cancer.

Dear God,

You are so great and powerful. I am in awe when I look at the stars, and I am grateful that in all that vastness You hear me when I question and doubt. What comforting reassurance to know that You care for me so much You call me by Your own special name. Thank You for being with me through this cancer.

In Jesus' name, amen

May God's mighty power comfort you today.

5

HOLD ON!

Holding On to God's Hand with Hopeful Relief

*Let us hold unswervingly to the hope we profess,
for he who promised is faithful.*
~ Hebrews 10:23

I remember the last time I rode a roller coaster (and I mean the last time). My husband and I had taken a group of kids to Six Flags over Texas in Arlington, Texas. My husband, the adventurous one, coerced me into riding with him on the Texas Giant, the largest roller coaster in the park. Under much protest, I climbed into the two-seated car, tightly grasped the bar that came down over us, and firmly set my feet to brace myself for the anticipated tortuous ride.

As we topped the first tall incline, I thought, "This is a nice view." Then in panic, I squeezed my eyes closed as we careened straight down the other side of the incline and flew around a death-defying curve. As the car slowed slightly and climbed up another hill, I briefly caught my breath; but as if mocking my white knuckles, the coaster hurdled us back down and around another curve. Feeling out of control, swerving madly up and down hills and around curves, I screamed, "When will this be over?"

After what seemed like 30 minutes instead of the actual 3, we coasted to a safe stop, and I felt secure enough to open my eyes. With immense relief the "joy ride" was over. I joyously walked away (on very wobbly legs) strongly vowing to my husband, "I will never ride a roller coaster again!" I unswervingly held on to the hope that after I boldly approached my husband concerning my feelings about any future roller coaster rides, he would faithfully promise not to ask again.

I have often compared my journeys with cancer to that experience. I protested, "I do not want cancer!" It felt frightening and death defying. Just when I thought I could handle it all, my emotions would suddenly swerve up and down and around again. In panic times I wanted to scream out, "When will it be over?" It seemed to last such a long, long time, and my life felt out of control. Weak and wobbly physically and emotionally, I was relieved and joyful when it was all over.

What got me through the roller coaster rides with cancer? Holding on to the hope I profess in Jesus Christ who, through His crucifixion and resurrection, made a way for me—and you—to go boldly to God with our fears and protests. He promises to faithfully "hold on" to us. What a relief!

For I am the Lord, your God,
who takes hold of your right hand and says to you,
Do not fear; I will help you.
~ Isaiah 41:13[1]

Dear God,

I am holding on to Your hand today. Thank You that I don't have to be afraid because You are here to help me through the ups and downs of the cancer coaster.

In Jesus' name I pray, amen.

Encouraging you to keep holding on.

6

SPARKLES FOR YOUR DAY

Glimmering with God's Sparkles of Abundant Blessings

> *Our light and momentary troubles
> are achieving for us an eternal glory
> that far outweighs them all.*
>
> ~ 2 Corinthians 4:17

Can cancer be a blessing? I did not believe so when in 1998 I was diagnosed with breast cancer—my third journey with cancer, having been treated twice for lymphoma in the early seventies. Coming at a dark and challenging time when my husband had lost his job and we were making plans to move to Oxford, Ohio, we struggled with trying to make sense out of what appeared nonsensical. What we could not understand at the time is that God was using my experiences with cancer to work out a divine plan for us to be a blessing and receive sparkles of blessings in return.

Like a diamond hidden in rock, undergoing centuries of pressure to form its sparkling beauty, I felt I was being squeezed and molded during that dark time. My husband and I wrestled with accepting the diagnosis and making decisions about treatments. During the uncertain time of tests and surgeries and the long arduous period of chemotherapy, God began the painful process of cutting and chipping the rough diamond that He saw in me to reveal hidden sparkles that would shine out blessings to others.

While searching for answers, I started journaling. The journaling led to writing devotional thoughts that led to developing inspirational cards. I shared these cards with other patients at the oncology clinic where I received my treatments, and sparkles of blessings began to brighten my journey.

On one occasion, I met with a lady who had just been diagnosed with an advanced stage of cancer. She was alone waiting in the exam room. At first she was reserved and assured me she was doing alright. I shared with her a bit then handed her a packet of cards. She laid them down on the exam table, then turned around and grabbed me in a bear hug, sobbing. We hugged and cried together. A big sparkle was added to my diamond.

A few weeks later, the nurse at the clinic told me this patient had passed away. "Her family was so touched by your kindness, they wanted you to have this," handing me an envelope with a donation and thank you. Another sparkle added.

Is cancer a blessing? If I had my choice, I would rather receive blessings through less painful and difficult ways. But that was not God's supreme plan. He saw a diamond that needed to be refined and used cancer as His tool.

Sparkles are emerging from this rough diamond, but the chipping process continues. Without going through three journeys with cancer and now living with chronic illnesses as a result of chemotherapy, I would not be able to relate encouragement to others with illness. So I keep shining out blessings where I can and look for sparkles of blessings to return to me.

As you read this, you are giving my ministry another sparkle! God bless you.

Do you feel like you are being squeezed, chipped, and chiseled during your illness? It may be hard, but it's okay. Let God, the Master jeweler, refine and polish you into His special sparkling creation. And in the process, look for glimmering sparkles of blessings to brighten your journey!

We can *"be joyful in hope, patient in affliction, faithful in prayer,"*[1] because *"our light and momentary troubles are achieving for us an eternal glory that far outweighs them all."*[2]

Dear God,

I'm so glad you see a diamond in me. Help me trust in Your refining work even when it hurts. Thank You for giving me sparkles of hope and blessings.

In Jesus' name I pray, amen.

My Reflections

He LOVES ME!

7

You're the Apple of My Eye

Confident in God's Loving Protection

Guard me as the apple of your eye.
~ Psalm 17:8

I tried my best to hold my eyes open and not blink while the ophthalmologist peered into my dilated pupils with his bright light. After the examination, as I blinked away the spots, he told me my eyes looked healthy and to come back in a year.

No, he did not find any apples in my eyes, so what does this verse "apple of your eye" mean? When I think of an apple, I see an image of a juicy fruit. In this instance, however, the term "apple" refers to the pupil in the center of the eye because of its round shape. The pupil is the hole that, like a window, allows light to land on the retina, producing the images we see around us. Because eyelids automatically close in protection of the eye when there is danger, like curtains, the eye became a symbol in ancient Hebrew culture representing something so precious it needs protection. That something is sight.[1]

Although David, the psalmist, may not have had a full understanding about the anatomy of the eye, he understood its symbolic significance. In faith, he cried out to the Lord for help, knowing that he was as precious to the Lord as the Lord's very own eyes: *Guard me as the apple of your eye.*

He Loves Me!

It was a prayer of faith that just as the Lord protects His own precious vision, the Lord would watch over and protect David.[2]

And perhaps, it was also a prayer of confident faith in the radiance of the Lord's love filling David's heart. Just as light enters the open pupil of the eye to give us sight of the physical elements around us, so the light of the Lord radiates into our open hearts to give us insight of His presence in the midst of our circumstances.

We know that when we are in an extreme emotional situation such as fear or pain, the pupil of our eyes dilates, strengthening our sight. And when we are in an extreme stressful situation like the diagnosis of cancer, it is time to open the windows of our hearts wider so the power of the Lord's love shines more brightly into our hearts, giving us the strength we need.

Are you feeling overwhelmed by your cancer diagnosis? Eat an apple. Let it remind you that you are very precious in the Lord's eyes and that He is watching over you. You can confidently open the window of your heart to let His bright light of love, hope, and comfort shine in and fill you with His peace.

Dear Lord,

Like David, I pray in confident faith that You are guarding and protecting me through my journey with cancer. Thank You for watching over me. I need a refuge of Your strength and comfort, so I open up the window of my heart. Please fill it with the bright light of Your peace and love.

In Jesus' name I pray, amen.

Enjoy an apple today, confident in the Lord's care.

8

HE LOVES ME
HE LOVES ME NOT

God is love
~ 1 John 4:16

"He loves me, he loves me not. He loves me, he loves me not," I repeated as I plucked the petals off a daisy. This was always a fun way to predict the youthful affections of my current heartthrob. When the last plucked petal revealed that he loved me, my heart leaped. Of course, the predictions never proved reliable.

Fortunately, predictions of God's love, a love that never fails, are reliable. This was a message the people of Israel needed to hear. The northern tribes of Israel had been captured by the Assyrians in 722 B.C. and sent into exile from their homeland. Discouraged, they questioned and doubted God's love. Had God abandoned them?

For over 200 years throughout their time of exile, God's love was watching over them. He sent this message of reassurance through the prophet Jeremiah,

I have loved you with an everlasting love;
I have drawn you with unfailing kindness.

~ Jeremiah 31:3

God's love was working to draw His people into a closer relationship with Him and give them hope for their future. The Message Bible translates Jeremiah 31:3 as, "God told them, 'I've never quit loving you and never will. Expect love, love, and more love!'" WOW! His love was inexhaustible, unchanging, perfect, total, and forever, despite their situation or the circumstances that led to their exile.

When I was diagnosed with cancer for the third time, my husband and I felt exiled from the life we had known and abandoned by God's love. Through the trials and emotions of tests, surgeries, treatments, and now chronic illnesses, we have continually seen and felt the unfailing love of God drawing us into a closer, deeper relationship with Him, a relationship that gives us hope for our future with Him through Jesus Christ.

God's message of unfailing love is the same for you today, despite the situation or circumstances of your illness. He will draw you into a love relationship with Him—one that is inexhaustible, unchanging, perfect, total, and forever. So you can confidently pluck the petals off a daisy and say . . .

He loves me, He loves me, He loves me . . .

He loves me!

Dear God,

I haven't always been confident of Your love since I was diagnosed with cancer. I have felt abandoned and exiled like the people of Israel. Thank You that You still keep loving me even when I doubt and question. And thank You that because You love me with such an inexhaustible everlasting love, I can have hope for my future because of Your Son Jesus Christ.

In Jesus' name, amen.

WOW! Be reassured. God loves you.

9

My Heart Is How Big?

God Measures the Heart with Warm Assurance

*People look at the outward appearance,
but the LORD looks at the heart.*

~ 1 Samuel 16:7

"Tachycardia what?" I asked the cardiologist after undergoing a couple of days of tests on my heart to determine what was causing the occasional pounding heartbeats I felt. "It sounds like a lion, it feels like a lion, but it is really a lamb," the cardiologist replied. "It will probably go away on its own. If not, we can prescribe some medication to control it." He was right; it did go away, and I have had no more problems. I wish all my heart issues were resolved that easily, especially the ones the Lord looks at.

The cardiologist looked at and measured my physical heart, but the Lord looks at and measures my spiritual heart. Does He feel dismay when He sees me feeling anxious over my health issues and my past cancer diagnoses, or when I get impatient with the little old lady in front of me at the checkout line who is taking her time moving out of my way? Does He feel joy when He sees me showing compassion to another cancer patient who is having a bad day, or when I spend time reading the Bible and talking to Him in prayer? In spite of the times He must feel dismay, I hope when the Lord looks at and measures my heart that He sees a woman after His own heart.

What did the Lord see when He looked at and measured the heart of the psalmist David?

When David was a young shepherd, God called the prophet Samuel to go to the home of David's father to anoint the new king of Israel. Each time Samuel met one of David's seven brothers, Samuel thought that he must be the Lord's choice. But the Lord said to Samuel, *"For the Lord sees not as man sees: man looks on the outward appearance, but the Lord looks on the heart."*[1] When Samuel met David, the Lord told him, *"Arise, anoint him, for this is he."*[2] From the beginning, the Lord found David to be *"a man after His own heart."*[3]

David served God faithfully as king, but he also brought dismay to God's heart. David had an adulterous affair with Bathsheba and caused the murder of her husband after David learned that she was pregnant with his child. Confronted by Nathan with his sin, David's heart was broken before the Lord. Even though the Lord must have felt dismay over David's sins, He looked on David's heart with love. David wrote in Psalm 86:5,

> *For you, O Lord, are good and forgiving,*
> *abounding in steadfast love to all who call upon you.*

We will stumble and fall along the way and bring dismay to the Lord's heart. Each time we fall and call to Him saying, "I am sorry," what will He see when He looks at and measures our hearts? Will He see a heart that is truly after His own heart?

I will continue trying day by day to keep my heart after the Lord's heart while I stumble along. As I spend time with Him, I pray He will help me be more patient with the little old ladies in the checkout lines, to trust Him more when I am feeling anxious about my health issues, and to bring more joy to His heart.

Because I am assured of His forgiveness and love through Jesus Christ, I know that I am "the one" in His heart. And so are you. You are the one He is compassionate about; you are the one He loves; you are the one He longs to hold through your cancer journey.

Lord,

Thank You that You still love me even when I stumble and fall. I'm grateful for Your forgiveness every time I call to You. Help me to have Your heart as I trust in Your care with this cancer diagnosis.

In Jesus' name, amen.

My Reflections

He Loves Me!

10

WHAT A SKY

*Holding on with Amazing Peace
in God's Divine Fingers*

> When I look at your heavens, the work of your fingers,
> the moon and the stars which you have set in place,
> what is man that you are mindful of him,
> and the son of man that you care for him?
> Yet you have made him a little lower than the heavenly beings and
> crowned him with glory and honor.
>
> ~ Psalm 8:3–5

One of my fondest memories is the week each year that I spent at camp in the mountains of New Mexico. I can still feel the crispness of the mountain air and smell the fresh aroma of pine trees. One night during the week, we would move our sleeping bags out of the cabin, place them by a campfire, and settle in for an evening of singing and telling stories. As the fire died down, we quietly snuggled into our sleeping bags and laid back to gaze at the night sky.

What a sky! Like a crown of precious jewels placed above our heads, the night sky dazzled with the brilliance of the moon surrounded by thousands of sparkling stars. The moon seemed close enough to reach out and touch. It captured our imaginations and held us in awe, as we considered the work of God's fingers.

The divine fingers that ordained the moon and the stars are the same fingers that made you. The divine fingers that crown the night sky with heavenly jewels are the same fingers that crown you with glory and honor. The divine fingers that hold the moon and stars in place are the same fingers that faithfully hold you in His loving care. How amazing!

Consider the work of God's divine fingers. Find strength and peace in the assurance of His intimate presence with you as you face the trials and challenges of your journey with cancer.

Dear God,

Thank you for the assurance that You are mindful of me and caring for me during this time with cancer. What amazing peace to know You are holding me with Your divine fingers through each step of this journey.

In Jesus' name I pray, amen.

Praying you feel God's divine fingers

11

I Am Wonderfully Made

Confident in God's Faithful Care

The next time you admire all the wonderful things God has made . . . remember you are the best of them!

Did you know . . .

- Human bone is as strong as granite in supporting weight. A block of bone the size of a matchbox can support nine tons.
- The focusing muscles of the eyes move around 100,000 times a day. To give your leg muscles the same workout, you would need to walk 50 miles every day.
- You use 200 muscles to take one step.
- Nerve impulses to and from the brain travel as fast as 170 mph. Operating on the same amount of power as a 10-watt light bulb, the human brain can hold 5 times as much information as the Encyclopedia Britannica.
- Every day the average person loses 60–100 strands of hair. (Unless, you are taking chemotherapy!)
- The human heart creates enough pressure to squirt blood 30 feet. The body is estimated to have 60,000 miles of blood vessels.
- The lungs contain over 300,000 million capillaries. If they were laid end to end, they would stretch 1,500 miles.
- Scientists have counted over 500 different liver functions.
- Your nose can remember 50,000 different scents.

- Coughs clock in at about 60 mph. Sneezes regularly exceed 100 mph. God bless you!
- Of the estimated 10–50 trillion cells in the body, 300 million cells die in the human body every minute. Every day an adult body produces 300 billion new cells.
- About 32 million bacteria call every inch of your skin home. (Eww!) A majority of these are entirely harmless and some are even helpful in maintaining a healthy body.

Did you know when you awake with the discomforts of cancer, God knows them all and is ready to help you? Or when you awake feeling better and have a good day, God is smiling with you?[1] He is thinking about you all day. He knows every hair on your head,[2] every muscle you use, every dying cell and every new cell, every heart beat,[3] and every breath.[4]

Did you know when parts of His wonderfully complex creation do not function as He designed, God is working on your behalf to bring about good for a purpose?[5] When we question why, God says to trust Him.[6] *"My gracious favor is all you need. My power works best in your weakness."*[7]

You are God's special creation. He cares very deeply about you and what you are facing with cancer. *"If God cares so wonderfully for flowers that are here today and gone tomorrow, won't he more surely care for you?"*[8]

So the next time you sneeze, let it be an encouraging reminder that God is watching over you. God bless you!

Dear God,

Thank you for making me so wonderfully complex! Your workmanship is marvelous—and how well I know it. How precious are your thoughts about me, O God! They are innumerable! I can't even count them; they outnumber the grains of sand! And when I wake in the morning, you are still with me! In Jesus' name I pray, amen.

12

A Warm Smile *from* God's Love

. . . makes a cheerful countenance.
~ Proverbs 15:13

We're poked and prodded, cut and stuck, snipped and snapped in places we didn't know existed on our bodies. We learn a new language and meet countless people whose names we cannot remember. We question and we trust; we cry and we laugh; we fear and we hope. We take notes, mark our calendars, and alter our to-do lists. We are forced into a lifestyle totally foreign to us after being diagnosed with cancer.

Having a merry heart is not exactly a high priority on our agendas! Yet, as we read in Proverbs, "He who is of a merry heart has a continual feast" and "a merry heart does good, like medicine."

We could certainly use a continual feast of good medicine to help us through our journey with cancer. How do we make our hearts feel happy and cheerful when carrying such heavy loads? Perhaps, we can start by turning the verse in Proverbs 15:13 around—*"A cheerful countenance makes a merry heart."*

Smiles are contagious and have been called the universal medicine. We can take a smile into every situation we face each day. Yes, it is easy to smile when we consider that *"neither death nor life, nor angels nor principalities nor powers, nor things present nor things to come, nor height nor depth, nor any other created thing, shall be able to separate us from the love of God which is in Christ Jesus our Lord."*[1]

Dear God,

My heart hasn't felt much like smiling since I was diagnosed with cancer. A continual feast of good medicine would be a blessing. So I ask You to tug at the corners of my mouth as You remind me how much You love me. Then, help me to share that smile with someone else.

In Jesus' name, amen.

May you feel the embrace of God's warm smiles today.

13

SING!

Trusting in God's Bountiful Love and Mercy

> *How long, O Lord? Will you forget me forever?*
> *How long will you hide your face from me?*
> *How long shall I take counsel in my soul,*
> *Having sorrow in my heart daily?*
> *How long will my enemy be exalted over me?*
>
> ~ Psalm 13:1–2

Israel's most prominent king was David, known as a man after God's own heart. He wrote much of the book of Psalms, many of which are expressions of his anguish during times when enemies seeking his death pursued him.

David begins Psalm 13 with agonizing questions, wrestling over what appears to be God's lack of response to attacks from his enemy. But then he concludes the song by saying,

> *But I have trusted in Your mercy;*
> *My heart shall rejoice in Your salvation.*
> *I will sing to the Lord,*
> *Because He has dealt bountifully with me.*[1]

He Loves Me!

Rejoice and sing? What can David find to sing about? Why does he want to sing when an enemy is pursuing him seeking his life? Is this being "dealt bountifully"? David seems to need a reality check!

As David cried out to the Lord, the apparent reality of his circumstances began to fade in the light of the true reality of God's faithfulness. David's reason to sing was in the reality that God's bountiful grace and mercy would carry him through the struggles with his enemies and assure him of God's salvation. That was David's reality check!

Do you identify with David's questioning of God as you wrestle with similar issues over attacks from cancer? Do you question, "Am I being dealt bountifully?" Like David, as you pray to the Lord with your questions and concerns, you, too, will be able to see beyond the circumstances of this illness to the reality of God's unfailing love.

Yes, you can sing—with your voice or with your heart—because you can believe and trust that God's bountiful love, grace and mercy will carry you through this struggle. And when you declare your faith, you have the certainty of the promise of God's salvation through his Son Jesus Christ for this life and the next. That is your reality check!

Lord,

I understand David's pleading because this is how I feel sometimes during my journey with cancer. As I cry out to You, help me see the reality of You dealing bountifully with me in the midst of all I am facing. Put a song in my heart so I can confidently declare my faith in Your Son. Thank You for Your faithful love to me.

In Jesus' name, amen.

I will sing to my Lord a new song . . .

His Promises
ARE FOR ME FOREVER

14

Take Me Out
to the Ballgame

*For God so loved the world that he gave his one
and only Son, that whoever believes in him
shall not perish but have eternal life.
For God did not send his Son into the world to condemn
the world, but to save the world through him.*

~ John 3:16–17

"And it's One, Two, Three strikes you're out at the old ballgame"—so the song and the rules of the game go. I'm glad God doesn't play by the rules of baseball.

When I was diagnosed with cancer for the third time in 1998, feelings of fear, devastation, anger, confusion, and uncertainty intermingled with attempts at bravery and positive thinking. Questions with no apparent answers were directed to a God who did not appear to be present or even care. My husband and I cried and prayed and searched God's Word for reassurance.

As my treatments progressed, my health continued to deteriorate, and my eternity seemed to grow closer. Our desperate need and desire for God's love, hope, and comfort magnified. Gradually, the realization of an ever-present, loving God, who was bringing me through the trials for a purpose, grew brighter.

His Promises Are for Me Forever

Over thirteen years later I'm still in the ballgame. I continue to question and learn. I don't fully understand why I have been restored to health while some of my friends have finished their ballgames and gone home with the Lord. When my ballgame is over and I have gone home, then I am sure I'll understand.

Of one thing I am certain—no matter what the diagnosis or prognosis, whether we're still playing the game or about to strike out, when our faith is in God's Son, Jesus Christ, we are victorious through the promise of His Word.

Dear God,

Thank You for loving me so much that You sent Your Son, Jesus Christ, to die for my sins and then rise from death so I can live with You forever. I don't understand it, but I trust in Your promise. No matter how things might look today on this cancer journey, I know I can look forward to tomorrow with hope.

In Jesus' name, amen.

May you have many innings in your ballgame.

15

WHEN IT RAINS,
IT POURS AND POURS AND POURS

Standing Securely on God's Sure Foundation

> *When you go through deep waters and great trouble,*
> *I will be with you. When you go through rivers of*
> *difficulty, you will not drown!*
>
> ~ Isaiah 43:2

Our old house in Darrtown, OH, hints of life when it was built in 1866. Uneven wood plank floors creak when we walk on them as if trying to tell us a story from the past. The basement stretches across the front section of the house with stone walls and heavy strong oak beams forming the main foundation. A dirt and stone floor and the stone walls keep it cool throughout the hottest summer, which made it a useful root cellar before the days of electricity. I can imagine it once lined with shelves of canned fruits and vegetables from the family garden. Today it serves as storage for old paint cans with a very functional and needed sump pump. Water-stained evidence suggests that water seepage has been a normal part of the life of this old root cellar.

One cold spring morning, dark clouds dropped a gloomy daylong rain, punctuated by sheets of relentless downpours. My husband, Joe, kept a watchful eye on our basement for any water seepage. All remained dry, and we went to bed confident that the drainage work Joe had done earlier in the year was working.

Heat-sensitive paper – avoid prolonged exposure to heat or light.

Ticket valid only for drawing date(s) shown. Fast Play prizes expire one year from purchase date. Draw Game prizes expire one year from draw date. Void if torn, incomplete, illegible or altered. Not responsible for lost or stolen tickets. Winning claims subject to official rules & regulations of the Pennsylvania Lottery, 1200 Fulling Mill Road, Middletown, PA 17057.

PROBLEM GAMBLING HELP: 1-800-GAMBLER (1-800-426-2537)
PA Lottery Toll-Free: 1-800-692-7481

PNN

02/04/17

RETAILER NUMBER   DATE PAID

78849944

PENNSYLVANIA LOTTERY - Benefits Older Pennsylvanians. Every Day.
DRAWING RESULTS: palottery.com or **1-877-282-4639**

NAME _____ PHONE _____
ADDRESS _____
CITY _____ STATE _____ ZIP _____
SIGNATURE _____
E-MAIL _____

Heat-sensitive paper – avoid prolonged exposure to heat or light.

Ticket valid only for drawing date(s) shown. Fast Play prizes expire one year from purchase date. Draw Game prizes expire one year from draw date. Void if torn, incomplete, illegible or altered. Not responsible for lost or stolen tickets. Winning claims subject to official rules & regulations of the Pennsylvania Lottery, 1200 Fulling Mill Road, Middletown, PA 17057.

PROBLEM GAMBLING HELP: 1-800-GAMBLER (1-800-426-2537)
PA Lottery Toll-Free: 1-800-692-7481

PNN

02/04/17

RETAILER NUMBER   DATE PAID

78849945

PENNSYLVANIA LOTTERY - Benefits Older Pennsylvanians. Every Day.
DRAWING RESULTS: palottery.com or **1-877-282-4639**

NAME _____ PHONE _____
ADDRESS _____
CITY _____ STATE _____ ZIP _____
SIGNATURE _____
E-MAIL _____

Heat-sensitive paper – avoid prolonged exposure to heat or light.

Ticket valid only for drawing date(s) shown. Fast Play prizes expire one year from purchase date. Draw Game prizes expire one year from draw date. Void if torn, incomplete, illegible or altered. Not responsible for lost or stolen tickets. Winning claims subject to official rules & regulations of the Pennsylvania Lottery, 1200 Fulling Mill Road, Middletown, PA 17057.

PROBLEM GAMBLING HELP: 1-800-GAMBLER (1-800-426-2537)
PA Lottery Toll-Free: 1-800-692-7481

PNN

02/04/17

RETAILER NUMBER   DATE PAID

www.palottery.com www.palottery.com www.palottery.com

Second Chance Prize Zone™
Official Entry Code
180TX Q72GY SH3I0 0N03Q S9MJN

BEAT THE HEAT SECOND CHANCE DRAWING
Enter by Aug. 2 for a chance to win up to $100,000! Visit palottery.com for details and to enter tickets.

Tue. Cash 5 3kpt. $200,000; Wed. Powerball 3kpt. $110 Mil.; Tue. Mega Mil. 3kpt. $375 Mil.; Tue. Match 6 3kpt. $1,040,000.

Today is a good day to play MEGA MILLIONS. The jackpot tonight is $375 MILLION! Please play responsibly.

Term: 48197
718-0000-2407263330-00

48f4426
Jul 17, 2018 15:33
$2.00 - 1 Draw
Tue 17-Jul-2018
Megaplier No

A. 16 21 32 36 56 Megaball: 21 QP

Benefits Older Pennsylvanians, Every Day.

His Promises Are for Me Forever

Rain continued throughout the night, and early the next morning Joe checked the basement to find two feet of water. The sump pump was not able to keep up with the rising water. Joe put on his oldest pair of tennis shoes, rolled up his pants legs, and sloshed through the frigid water to install another pump, then a third, and a fourth. When the rain finally stopped, the water level reached about four feet.

Water seeped right back in after each futile attempt at pumping it out. A longtime resident of Darrtown told us to quit trying to pump out the water. "When the water level drops below the bedrock, all the water in your basement will drain out." So understanding our neighbor's wisdom, we shrugged our shoulders and thought, "This house has been here for over 140 years on a sound and good foundation that has kept it standing strong through many flooded basements." It took about a month for water to quit seeping in, and then one day it all drained out as our neighbor said it would.

When you were diagnosed with cancer, it probably felt like cold rain seeping in and flooding the foundations of your life. Proverbs 24:3 from the Amplified Bible says, *"Through skillful and godly Wisdom is a house (a life, a home, a family) built, and by understanding it is established [on a sound and good foundation]."*[1]

The builders of our house used wisdom and understanding to build a foundation that would withstand many floods. How can you build a "sound and good foundation" that will stand strong against the flooding circumstances you encounter with a diagnosis of cancer? By trusting in God's sure foundation, Jesus Christ. You can be confident He will hold you securely in His refuge, strong through the flood.

Dear Jesus,

The cold floodwaters just seem to keep coming into my life since I was diagnosed with cancer. Help me to stand securely on the foundation of the promises in Your Word.

In Your name I pray, amen.

He promises me

16

LET GO, LET GOD

Believing in God's Uplifting Promises

Trust in the Lord with all your heart, And lean not on your own understanding; In all your ways acknowledge Him, And He shall direct your paths.

~ Proverbs 3:5

Tucked snugly into a soft, secure nest, weak vulnerable baby birds begin their lives totally trusting in the care of their parents. As the young birds grow and their wings gain strength, some bird parents will begin taking out the soft cushion lining of the nest to force the young birds closer to the edge. Encouraged to begin actively exercising their wings, the young birds are soon nudged over the side of the nest by their parent. They are forced to let go of their source of comfort and security, dramatically challenging their level of trust. Finding themselves suddenly falling, the young birds quickly rise to a new level of confidence as they learn to use their resources—the strength of their wings and an air current lifting them up.

Just as the young birds trusted in the comfort and security of their nest and in the daily care of their parents, we go through our lives trusting (often without thought) in the things that give us comfort and security: faith, family, homes, jobs, health. We find our level of confidence, like the young birds, dramatically challenged when the diagnosis of cancer forces us to let go of these things. We must learn to rise to a new level of dependent trust, believing in the strength of the Lord and His uplifting promises—a solid source of comfort and security.

Have faith in the Lord as you go through the journey with cancer. He promises,

> *Be strong and courageous, . . . for it is the Lord your*
> *God who goes with you.*[1]

Lean on the Lord as you make decisions about treatments. He promises,

> *I will instruct you and teach you in the way you should go;*
> *I will counsel you with my eye upon you.*[2]

Rely on the Lord through the challenges of eating properly while you are ill. Jesus promises,

> *Therefore do not be anxious, saying,*
> *"What shall we eat?" or "What shall we drink?". . .*
> *For . . . your Heavenly Father knows that you need them all.*[3]

Depend on the Lord when you are concerned about the welfare of your family. He promises,

> *I will set my eyes on them for good.*[4]

Rest in the Lord when your sleep is disturbed.

He promises,

> *If you lie down, you will not be afraid;*
> *when you lie down, your sleep will be sweet.*[5]

Confidently trust in the Lord for the future of your journey.

His Promises Are for Me Forever

He promises,

> *For I know the plans I have for you, declares the Lord, plans for welfare and not for evil, to give you a future and a hope.* [6]

Dear God,

Cancer has taken the soft cushion out of my nest and forced me to let go of some of the things that gave me comfort and security every day. It has been hard. Help me to rise to a new level of trust, to be able to let go and let You, God, take me through this journey day by day. I trust in Your promises.

In Jesus' name I pray, amen.

*My favorite promise from God is*___

17

POWERFUL! ALIVE!

Powerful Strength in God's Word

The grass withers, the flower fades
But the word of our God stands forever.
~ Isaiah 40:8

"I promise. Cross my heart and hope to die." Remember saying that as a kid? This emphatic statement was our assurance to someone that they could trust our word—a promise we may or may not have kept.

Nearly three thousand years ago, the prophet Isaiah served as God's voice to the nation of Judah admonishing, encouraging, and comforting them with God's promises. As the nation drew closer to the certainty of years of captivity, God gave an emphatic statement assuring them that although they would go through a period of difficult times, He would keep His promise to be with them. They could trust that His word would stand true.

And so can we. Although nations and peoples have withered and faded over the centuries, God's word has stood through time and today is still *"living and powerful."*[1]

God also kept His promise to Lorene that His word would stand forever. She was a brilliant woman, a college professor, who loved to read, especially God's Word. Over the last few years of her life, we watched her mind and body wither and fade from Alzheimer's. At her funeral the pastor related about his last visit

His Promises Are for Me Forever

with her as she lay on her deathbed. Lorene did not know who he was and spoke with garbled, unintelligible sounds. As the pastor began to recite Psalm 23, he heard Lorene's soft voice repeating the words with him. The word of God had stood living and powerful in Lorene even as her mind and body withered and faded.

When you feel withered and faded along your journey with cancer, trust in the promise that God's words can be living and powerful in you. The Bible is full of God's words of promises that you can hold in your heart to strengthen and help you through your difficult time. You wrote your favorite in the last devotional, now find more, such as Psalm 23 and write them on the next page. Feed on them until you feel them living and powerful in you. God faithfully promises that it will stand forever, reminding you that He is with you.

Dear God,

It's when I am feeling withered and faded that I most need Your promises to assure me that You are with me. Thank You that so many of the promises You gave many years ago have stood through all this time to help me today. They give me comfort and strength.

In Jesus' name, amen.

He promises me

I Will Fear Not
BUT TRUST

18

I Am

Comforting Power in the Lord's Presence

> Fear not, Abram [and ____your name____],
> I am your shield; your reward shall be very great.
> ~ Genesis 15:1

I like to travel, but I never wanted to take this journey.
This road was meant for someone else to travel, not me.
Now I am on this journey—this journey with cancer.

I wonder what is ahead for me? What will life be like?
I hear horror stories of what others have gone through, then
I see those who have traveled this road before me
    and completed the journey.
I am encouraged. I want to be brave and strong like them.
I am on a journey with cancer.

I pretend when I awake in the morning that it was just a
    bad dream, then
I touch the scars from surgery and I know it is real.
I worry about my family. How will they cope?
I cry from fear. I cry from anger.
I feel alone. Is God near? Does God care?
I am on a journey with cancer.

I understand there is no turning back. I must press forward.
I say, "I can do this. I will make it through to the end."

*I dream of the day when this will all be over and life will
    return to normal. Or will it?*
*I try to be positive and smile to everyone around me, so
    they won't know my deep inner struggles.*
*I hope God understands all my insecurities, my fears,
    my anxieties.*
I am on a journey with cancer.

Yes, God does understand and He is with you. You can trust in God's "I AM" presence and press forward with confidence declaring, "I am victorious on this journey with cancer."

I AM WHO I AM,"[1] God declared from the burning bush as He gave Moses instructions for leading the Israelites on a journey out of slavery from Egypt. In those simple words, God declared that He was the unchanging, all powerful, all knowing, all sufficient presence to be with them on their journey.

Journeys are prevalent throughout the Bible. God's *I AM* presence in each of these journeys has been preserved in the records of the Bible for our encouragement today.

I am your shield; your reward shall be very great.[2]

Behold, I am with you and will keep you wherever you go.[3]

*I am the Lord your God, who teaches you to profit, who leads you in the
    way you should go.*[4]

I, I am he who comforts you.[5]

Jesus declared His I AM presence during His journey on earth.

*I am the light of the world. Whoever follows me will never
    walk in darkness, but will have the light of life.*[6]

*I am the resurrection and the life. He who believes in me
    will live, even though he dies.*[7]

As Jesus was ready to take His final journey back to heaven, He commissioned His followers to journey out and tell the world about Him, reassuring them of His *I Am* presence.

And surely I am with you always, to the very end of the age.[8]

Yes, God does understand. And He is with you. You can trust in God's "I AM" presence and press forward with confidence declaring,

I am victorious on this journey with cancer.

I am on a victorious pilgrimage . . .

I Wil Fear Not, but Trust

19

It's Cool

Warm Refuge in God's Gift of Peace

*I am leaving you with a gift —
peace of mind and heart.*
~ John 14:27

Time for another routine checkup. I still don't feel routine about these visits with my doctor although it's been several years since my last chemo treatment. The feelings of apprehension and thoughts of "what if" still haunt me.

Does it mean that I am lacking in my faith and trust in the loving watchful care of my heavenly Father? Absolutely not! Does it mean that my emotions are very real and acceptable to God? Absolutely yes!

A few years ago, I felt thrust out of my normal world and back into the world of being a cancer patient when I was scheduled for a routine bone scan. As the technicians poked around on my arm for my elusive one vein needed to give me the injection for the bone scan, my stomach knotted, and I experienced flashbacks of the time I was in treatment. All the words of encouragement I have been sharing became very personal.

I was reassured of God's presence during my bone scan. Imagine having a spiritual moment in nuclear medicine! The technician was busy at the computer and the room was quiet with soft music playing. As I lay on the table (perfectly still of course) with

I Will Fear Not, but Trust

the scanner inches above my nose, I closed my eyes and shared with God all the emotions and doubts I was experiencing.

A picture came into my mind of a young man dressed casually in blue jeans sitting on top of the scanner with his legs crossed. He was smiling down at me and reassured me, "It's cool." An angel? I like to think so. I know that it gave me a tremendous sense of peace.

Peace is the gift that Jesus gave his disciples when they were feeling troubled and unsure over what Jesus had been saying about leaving them, as he was preparing them for his impending crucifixion and resurrection.

> *And the peace I give isn't like the peace the world gives.*
> *So don't be troubled or afraid.*
>
> *~ John 14:27*

My bone scan and tests were all good that year. This year I know that whatever my doctor tells me about the results of my tests, as I share my unsure feelings with Jesus, I will have the assurance of his gift of peace.

And so can you. Whatever uncertainties cause you to feel apprehensive and unsure about your diagnosis, trust in your safe haven, Jesus, to give you peace of mind and heart.

Lord Jesus,

Sometimes I not only feel troubled but afraid. I try to be hopeful with every test, but "what if" keeps nagging at me. Help me to trust in the promise you gave your disciples, peace of mind and heart. Thank You for being with me through this journey with cancer.

Amen.

Remember, it's cool with God!

20

SAVE ME, LORD!

The Power of Faith in Times of Trouble

Don't be afraid. . . . Take courage, I am here.
~ Matthew 14:27

"Help! Save me!" Edward yelled to Joe, frantically splashing his arms around attempting to keep his head above water. My husband, Joe, instantly grabbed his fishing net which had a long rope attached and flung it toward Edward. Just as he was about to go under the water, Edward caught hold of the rope; coughing and shivering, he was pulled to safety.

Edward was one of our boys in a group home where we worked and lived as teaching parents. Joe had taken the boys fishing at the local river and given them strict instructions to stay away from the steep bank. Edward, however, did not stay focused on Joe's safety instructions and wandered to the river bank. When he found himself in trouble, Edward cried out to his *life saver*, Joe.

When the disciple Peter found himself in trouble, he cried out to his *Life Saver*, Jesus. Peter and the other disciples were in a boat crossing the Sea of Galilee late one night when strong winds whipped up large waves crashing around their boat.

Jesus saw that they were in trouble and came to them, *"walking on the [stormy] water."*[1] When he recognized that it was Jesus, "Peter called to him, 'Lord, if it's really you, tell me to come to you *by walking on water.' 'All right, come,' Jesus said. So Peter went over the side of the boat and walked on the water toward Jesus. But when he looked around at the high waves, he was terrified and began to sink. 'Save me, Lord!' he shouted. Instantly, Jesus reached out his hand and grabbed him."*[2]

With trusting faith, Peter focused on Jesus' instruction to "come"; then he got out of the boat and walked toward Jesus. But when he took his eyes off Jesus and saw the stormy conditions around him, Peter's faith faltered, and he began to sink. As soon as he refocused his faith on Jesus, his *Life Saver*, and cried out, Peter was lifted up to safety and returned to the boat.

The Bible does not tell us how they got back into the boat, only that they did. I like to think that Jesus held on to Peter's hand, and they walked back together on the water to the boat.

Do you feel overwhelmed by the diagnosis of cancer, like you are sinking in the midst of waves crashing around you? Jesus' instruction to you is, "Come." Have faith in your Life Saver, Jesus. He will lift you up above the stormy waves so you can walk on water. When the waves start to overwhelm you and you feel your faith faltering as you begin to sink, refocus on Jesus. Shout as Peter did, "Save me, Lord!" Tell him what you are afraid of on the next pages. Jesus will reach out and grab you; He will hold on to you as you walk together over the stormy waves to the completion of your journey with cancer.

Dear Jesus,

There have been many sinking days since cancer came into my life. Tests, surgery, needles, pain, and sickness come in waves crashing around me while waves of fear, anxiety, uncertainty, and anger threaten to drown me. I need You to grab hold of me and lift me up. I want to walk on these stormy waters with You, so I'm shouting, SAVE ME, LORD!

In Your name I pray, amen.

Save me Lord, _____

21

Trouble Lurking About

Strengthened by God's Ever-Present Help

> *God is our refuge and strength,*
> *an ever-present help in trouble.*
>
> ~ Psalm 46:1

The dry warmth of our 150-year old house beckoned a stray mouse to seek refuge from the cold, much to the delight of our cat. My husband and I were relaxing in our living room visiting with friends when we heard a commotion in the dining room. We looked in to witness a mouse race across the floor with our cat, Jingles, in close pursuit. Mousy darted under the protection of the buffet just in time to avoid a swipe of Jingles' bared claws. As Mousy peeked out from the other side of the buffet, the frantic chase resumed—under the table, around the chairs, back under the buffet, then sprinting into the kitchen.

Quickly slipping under the refrigerator, Mousy found protection from the danger of Jingles' claws. While Jingles was preoccupied pawing as far as he could reach under the refrigerator to get to Mousy, Mousy took the opportunity to slip out the other side. It stopped by the stove and looked back at Jingles as if it was making sure that it had Jingles' attention, and then the cat and mouse game began again—under the stove, out the other side, across the kitchen floor, back into the dining room, under the table, around the chairs, under the buffet, out the other side, and dashing across the floor into the living room.

I Will Fear Not, but Trust

My friend and I squealed, quickly pulling up our feet onto the sofa, as Mousy scurried under the shelter of the coffee table in front of us. With head down and tail swishing in the air, Jingles intently surveyed the situation under the coffee table, while Mousy quietly slipped out the other side and ran across the floor. It stopped in front of the fireplace, sat up, and watched Jingles at the coffee table, as if saying, "Hey cat, over here!"

With a little help from us, Jingles soon was back in the pursuit—through the living room, into the dining room, under the table, around the chairs, under the buffet, across the floor, with Mousy finally disappearing into the furnace room. That was the last we saw of Mousy. When we went to bed, Jingles was dutifully on watch at the furnace room door.

Although Mousy's trouble remained lurking about, it knew where to find its refuge. Refuge is a shelter or protection from danger or distress, a means of resort for help in difficulty. Mousy's protection and shelter during the dangers of the chase helped give it the strength and confidence to boldly face its troubles with Jingles.

Many times during my journeys with cancer, I felt distressed and in need of protection from the dangers of the illnesses. Where did I find my refuge, my resort for help with my difficulties? When I spent time reading God's Word and praying, I found a renewed strength and confidence to boldly face my troubles with cancer.

And so can you. God cares about the dangers you face with cancer. You can trust in His word that He is your *ever-present help in trouble.*

Dear God,

Sometimes I feel like Mousy, with my troubles of cancer always lurking about. So I am asking for Your help and strength to boldly face this danger, trusting that *"You are my refuge and my shield; I have put my hope in your word."*[1]

In Jesus' name I pray, amen.

22

I'M GONNA GETCHA!

Hopeful Trust in God's Reassuring Word

In God, whose word I praise, in God I trust;
I shall not be afraid.

~ Psalm 56:4

October is especially full of man-made attempts to provoke fear; yet, thrill-seeking screams often morph into shrieks of laughter as the masks come off and the lights turn on.

Real-life fear, however, is no laughing matter.

The psalmist David was well-acquainted with real-life fear, as he expressed in Psalm 56. He was being pursued by his enemy, Saul, the insanely jealous king of Israel. In desperation, David fled to the city of Gath, the hometown of the Philistine giant, Goliath, whom David had heroically killed. When David wrote this psalm, he found himself surrounded by two enemies: King Saul and the Philistines. Fervently, David cried out to God, "Be gracious to me, O God, for man tramples on me; all day long an attacker oppresses me."

Then David declared, *"What time I am afraid, I will have confidence in and put my trust and reliance on You."*[1] Throughout the psalm, as David lamented over his enemies, he calmed his fears by reassuring himself he could trust and rely on God.

I remember well in 1998 when fear overwhelmed me. I had what I expected to be a routine mammogram, but the report from

I Will Fear Not, but Trust

the radiologist showed there was a growth and I needed to see a surgeon. All of a sudden it felt as though an attacker was trampling on me and oppressing my life.

I went home in shock and threw my arms around my husband crying, "I am so afraid!" Memories of what I experienced twenty years earlier when I endured very harsh treatments for Hodgkin's disease engulfed me in panic and despair.

Through that experience and many others over the past few years, I have been learning how to calm my fears and put my trust in God. This does not come instantly or easily and is not a one-time permanent cure. In many of David's psalms he kept reassuring himself that he could trust and rely on God, and so must I.

There are several Scripture verses I return to often to build my faith: *Romans 8:39, Psalm 18:2, Psalm 33:22, 2 Thessalonians 2:16–17, Isaiah 40:31, Matthew 28:20, Philippians 4:7, and Psalm 46:1.*

When you feel overwhelmed by the fearful circumstances of your illness, I encourage you to find your favorite verses. Write them down on the next page, memorize them, post them on your bathroom mirror, and carry them with you. Let them reassure you, calm you, and strengthen you, so you can, along with David, confidently say,

Lord,

The day I was told I had cancer I was afraid, very afraid. The immediate fear has subsided, but there are still times when I feel anxious. Help me to keep Your words close to my heart. I pray they will reassure me and calm my fears, so I can confidently say, "I trust in You." Thank You for being with me.

In Jesus' name I pray, amen.

---

*Praying you feel God's loving care
calming your fears.*

My Favorite Verses...

Putting His Gladness
IN MY HEART

23

It's So Unfair!

Hope in God's Bountiful Compassion

Why am I discouraged? Why is my heart so sad?
I will put my hope in God! I will praise him again--
my Savior and my God!

~ Psalm 42:11

I'm so angry! This cancer diagnosis is unfair. I don't deserve it. How could God let this happen? Is it okay to be angry? Does God understand my feelings? The Bible records numerous situations of anger and God's compassionate responses.

"*Cain was very angry, and his face fell.*"[1] This is the first recording of anger in the Bible. Cain, the firstborn of Adam and Eve, became angry when God accepted his brother Abel's offering but rejected his because it was not the best of *the fruit of the ground.*[2] So Cain, in jealous anger, killed his brother. God confronted Cain and chastised him, "*You shall be a fugitive and a wanderer on the earth.*"[3] When Cain pleaded with God about his fear of being killed, God in His mercy put a mark on Cain to prevent anyone from killing him. Cain had to learn a hard lesson about trusting God's faithful protection.

Moses had been in the holy presence of God on Mt. Sinai for forty days while God wrote with His finger on tablets of stone the law and the commandments. During that time the Israelites rebelled and built a golden calf to worship, thus inflaming Moses' righteous anger. "*As soon as he came near the camp and saw the calf and the dancing, Moses' anger burned hot, and he threw the tablets out of his hands and broke them at the foot of the mountain."*[4] God understood Moses' anger and rewrote His laws on new tablets for Moses to present to the people.

Time and time again, the Israelites also provoked the Lord's anger over their rebellion and unfaithfulness. *"For they have rejected the law of the Lord of hosts, and have despised the word of the Holy One of Israel. Therefore the anger of the Lord was kindled against his people."*[5] Although they had to bear the consequences of their actions, God repeatedly reached out to them with messages of hope if they would turn to Him in trust and faith.

Even Jesus expressed righteous anger toward the irreverence displayed in the Temple. *"And Jesus entered the temple and drove out all who sold and bought in the temple, and he overturned the tables of the money-changers and the seats of those who sold pigeons."*[6] Yet, believing in His Father's merciful love, Jesus continued healing and teaching those who came to Him.

That same love gives you hope today. Yes, it is okay to be angry about your illness. God does understand. All He asks is that you remain faithful to Him, trusting and relying on His bountiful compassion and care.

Dear God,

It is so hard to accept this diagnosis. I don't understand, but I thank You that You understand my feelings. Please help me trust and rely on You through this journey. I am grateful that *"You, O Lord, are a God of compassion and mercy, slow to get angry and filled with unfailing love and faithfulness. Look down and have mercy on me. Give your strength to your servant . . . for You, O Lord, help and comfort me."*[7]

In Jesus' name I pray, amen.

May you experience God's love and compassion today.

24

If Only . . .

Comfort for Anxious Times

*Be anxious for nothing,
but in everything by prayer and supplication, with thanksgiving,
let your requests be made known to God.*
~ Philippians 4:6

How often I have wished for a quick repair to a difficult situation—*If only I could win the lottery and repair my checkbook balance. If only I could forgive easier and repair relationships. If only I could take one pill and repair the cancer cells. If only . . . then I would not feel so anxious.*

Philippians 4:6 tells us to "be anxious for nothing." The original word used for anxious suggests a distraction, a preoccupation with things causing worry and stress. Feeling anxious over my third diagnosis of cancer certainly preoccupied my life. Worried about my future and my family and stressed over what I would have to go through, I was distracted from performing daily responsibilities, from getting needed rest, from reaching out to family and friends, and from seeking God's help with a thankful heart. Throughout the journey when I was overwhelmed with anxious thoughts, I needed reminders of God's presence, to ask Him for help, and then thank Him for His promise of peace.

In the past, my husband and I worked in a treatment center with severely emotionally disturbed youth. We used point cards as part of their teaching plans from which the youth earned privileges. The points were referred to as "reminders"—tangible symbols to help the youth remember to use appropriate behavior.

When you have times of feeling overwhelmed with anxious thoughts during your journey with cancer, you may need some type of tangible symbol as a reminder to "let your requests be made known to God." Try carrying an object, such as a stone, in your pocket. Each time you reach into your pocket, let it remind you of the promise given in the next verse of Philippians:

> . . . and the peace of God, which surpasses all understanding, will guard your hearts and minds through Christ Jesus. (v. 7)

Dear God,

Sometimes the worry and stress over this cancer diagnosis overwhelms me. I have trouble sleeping, focusing on daily routines, and sharing my feelings with my family. I want to rest in the special peace You promise to give me, so I am asking You to help me with my need right now. I am trusting in Your faithful presence with me during my journey with cancer.

In Jesus' name I pray, amen.

May the peace of God be your constant companion through your journey as you trust in His promise.

25

PUTTING GLADNESS *in* MY HEART

You have put gladness in my heart.
~ Psalm 4:7

The summer day was perfect—comfortable warm temperature, beautiful blue sky dotted with soft white clouds, trees swaying in the gentle breeze. "It doesn't get any better," I thought as I swung on a tire swing while watching our grandsons chase each other around the playground. Gladness swelled in my heart.

The dictionary gives a good description of my moment of gladness in the park: happy, cheerful, lighthearted, joyful; freedom from care, worry, or discontent; a sense of well-being. Sounds good, but how does this describe life with a diagnosis of cancer? Do we need good health or a perfect summer day to feel gladness? How do we find gladness in the midst of the trials with cancer?

Psalm 4:7 says that God has filled our hearts with gladness. Some Bibles, say "joy." Gladness and joy are gifts from God to show us His love and compassion.

God's gift of gladness comes in different packages. Cards, flowers, and kind words of encouragement make us feel happy and cheerful. We also feel lighthearted and joyful when we complete a treatment or receive a positive report.

Putting His Gladness in My Heart

Freedom from care, worry, or discontent comes as we trust in the love, hope, and comfort from God. A sense of well-being in the abundance of God's presence throughout the cancer journey is gladness that endures in our hearts.

Dear God,

It's been hard to feel gladness since I was diagnosed with cancer. You said You will put gladness in my heart, so I am asking for You to squeeze my heart with Your gladness—happy, cheerful, lighthearted, joyful gladness in the midst of my trials with cancer. Open my eyes and my heart to see all the ways You give it to me. Thank You for being with me.

In Jesus' name, amen.

---

*Say a prayer and feel the gift
of God's gladness squeezing your heart.
Remember God loves you!*

26

Flowers are Smiles from God

Confident in God's Sovereign Control

The Lord reigneth; let the earth rejoice.
~ Psalm 97:1

Terrible, horrible, very bad days disrupt everyone's lives in varying intensities from traumatic to average. My most traumatic day was when I heard, "It's cancer," for the third time in my life. Let me share with you one of my "average" terrible, horrible, very bad days and what I learned that has helped even during traumatic days.

My head was throbbing from allergies when I got up.

The Lord reigneth; let the earth rejoice.

I looked out my kitchen window to see a growing mound of dirt—that pesky mole was heading right under my rose bush!

The Lord reigneth; let the earth rejoice.

Ouch! My knee was screaming at me as I limped down the stairs with a load of laundry.

The Lord reigneth; let the earth rejoice.

Yikes! A swarm of termites greeted me when I went into the storage room for detergent.

The Lord reigneth; let the earth rejoice.

My husband, who was a real estate agent, came home and informed me that two closings which had been scheduled that day were postponed, and one of the sellers wanted to cancel the deal.

The Lord reigneth; let the earth rejoice.

I took care of my 89 year old mother, who had Alzheimer's and a severe respiratory condition. This day she thought I was the nice lady who was paid to take care of her, not her daughter.

The Lord reigneth; let the earth rejoice.

Passing by our weeping crab apple tree as I went out to get the mail, I stopped. So gorgeous! Bees were humming busily amidst the abundant fragrant pink blossoms. *Flowers are indeed smiles from God*, I thought. Perhaps God gives us these smiles to remind us that He does reign over everything in His creation and is personally in control of you and me through good and bad, through health and sickness. Thinking about that made each incident throughout the day a little more bearable. As I got my mother ready for bed, she thanked me for being a "good nurse." I was able to just smile and give her a big hug.

The Lord reigneth; let the earth rejoice.

You may be dealing with many traumatic terrible, horrible, bad days right now. Be encouraged. There are still smiles all around you. The Lord gave them to you because He knew you would need them today.

The Lord reigneth; let the earth (and you and me) rejoice.

Dear Lord,

Some days really are terrible and hard to get through, especially now with this illness as my daily companion. Thank You for reminding me each time I see a flower that You are in control and I am not alone. Help me learn to trust You more each day as I go through this journey.

In Jesus' name I pray, amen.

The Lord reigneth; let the earth rejoice . . .

Daily Victory
GOD'S WAY

27

NEED A LITTLE SUNSHINE?

Give Praise!

*From the rising of the sun to its going down
The Lord's name is to be praised.*

~ Psalm 113:3

Flames danced merrily in our fireplace, dispelling winter's chill by spreading a cozy blanket of warmth over my husband and me as we relaxed with a bowl of popcorn and reflected on our blessings. At that time, my cancer was in remission, my husband had a steady job, and our bills were paid. Life felt very comfortable. It was easy to praise the Lord.

This was not the case a few years ago when I was diagnosed with breast cancer and my husband had lost his job. Praise did not come easy then. I did not want to praise; I felt there was nothing to give praise for. Yet this Scripture commands us to praise the name of the Lord all day long! That is a tall order when you have been diagnosed with a serious illness like cancer. But when we think about what the names of the Lord mean, praise comes easier.

Throughout the Bible God's intimate involvement in the lives of His people was expressed through the praise of His various names. When we praise the name of the Lord, we can experience His loving nature in the midst of the circumstances of illness.

Consider some of the Hebrew names used in praising the Lord.

- JEHOVAH-ROHI – God is our shepherd.
- JEHOVAH-JIREH – God is our provider.
- JEHOVAH-ROPHE – God is our healer, our restoration.
- JEHOVAH-NISSI – God is our banner, our deliverance.
- JEHOVAH-SHAMMAH – God is present with us.
- JEHOVAH-SHALOM – God is our peace.
- EL-SHADDAI – God is all sufficient and all bountiful—the source of all blessing, fullness, and fruitfulness.

God is blessed by our praises, delights in our praises, dwells in our praises, and manifests His power in our praises as the sun rises and sets on each day of our illnesses. Need a little sunshine? *Praise the name of the Lord!*

Dear Lord,

I have so many needs right now since I was diagnosed with cancer. I praise You because You are my shepherd watching over me. I praise You because You provide strength when I am weak. I praise You because You heal my broken heart. I praise You because You are present with me and deliver me from feeling alone. I praise You because You give me Your peace. I praise You because You are everything I need to take me through this journey and bring warm sunshine into my cold dark days.

In Jesus' name, amen.

May the warmth of God's love, hope, and comfort shine on you today.

28

BEEING A BUSY BEE

Confident in God's To-Do List

Be doers of the word, and not hearers only.
~ James 1:22

To do lists are great tools of organization. Wives create "honey-do" lists for their husbands that keep them busy getting chores done. Marking tasks off a list gives a satisfying feeling of accomplishment.

"To do" lists can also cause feelings of despair and frustration over not being able to accomplish even the simplest task when you are sick and weak with a serious illness like cancer. However, being a "doer of the word" provides sweet relief and soothing comfort, like honey to the body.

Honey adds a pleasing sweet taste to foods and drinks and also has many natural beneficial properties. It is pure and antiseptic and can be used to soothe skin irritations and sore throats, to quiet coughs, to reduce the body's susceptibility to infections and colds, and even to relieve a hangover!

Psalm 119:103 says, *"How sweet are your words to my taste; they are sweeter than honey."*[1] As honey benefits the body, consider the sweet benefits found in God's "honey-do" list in the following verses:

Daily Victory God's Way

*He will give you all you need from day to day
if you live for him and make the Kingdom of God
your primary concern.*

~ Matthew 6:33[2]

Tell God what you need, and thank him for all he has done. *If
you do this, you will experience God's peace.*

~ Philippians 4:6–7[3]

**Trust in the Lord with all your heart . . . Seek his will
in all you do,** *and he will direct your paths.*

~ Proverbs 3:5–6[4]

Then Jesus said, **"Come to me, all of you who are weary and
carry heavy burdens,** *and I will give you rest."*

~ Matthew 11:28[5]

So humble yourselves under the mighty power of God,
and in his good time he will honor you.

~ I Peter 5:6[6]

*No eye has seen, no ear has heard, and no mind has
imagined what God has prepared* **for those who love him.**

~ 1 Corinthians 2:9[7]

Dear God,

It is very difficult sometimes to continue doing while I am sick. Help me to focus every day on Your "honey-do" list, especially on the days my list has to wait—to humble myself and seek You first, to come to You and tell You when I am weary, to thank You, and to love You. Let me know Your peace, Your direction, Your rest. I look forward to what You have prepared for me.

In Jesus' name I pray, amen.

29

This Way?
or That Way?

Confident in God's Sure Direction

*A man's mind plans his way,
but the Lord directs his steps and makes them sure.*

~ Proverbs 16.9

Dark and early in the morning, we headed out from Cincinnati in our tractor-trailer unit to make a delivery in Detroit, MI. My husband, Joe, is a truck driver and I often have the opportunity to travel with him. Before we began our journey, Joe called the company for directions, entered the address in the GPS, and recorded our route on the map. One wrong turn with a tractor-trailer unit can lead a driver into a situation where he can literally be stuck, so accurate directions are vital.

Everything was going smoothly until we came to construction and a fork in the road that was not on our map and confused the GPS. Having to make a split-second decision, Joe took the road to the left. We had not gone far when the road narrowed, and we knew this was not correct. Fortunately, there was not much traffic, and Joe was able to find a parking lot big enough to turn around.

We were confused and unsure of the correct route, so Joe had to call the company for further directions. To be sure and confident of our route, we checked the new directions with the map and GPS and were soon on our way to our destination, pulling up to the dock to complete our delivery. What a relief!

We plan the paths and courses of our lives with hopes and expectations of traveling along smooth roads toward our destinations without any wrong turns. When a serious illness like cancer throws an unexpected detour or fork in the road, we can be confused and unsure and need to seek new direction. Wise counsel, maps, compasses, and GPS are all useful in finding directions when we are traveling. When traveling an unsure road with an illness, we need wisdom from family, friends, and doctors to help us make decisions about the directions of the paths of our treatments.

You can be sure and confident of your directions when you pray and read the Bible—your spiritual map, compass, and GPS. What a relief to know that no matter what bumps and detours cancer may bring along the way, the Lord has gone before you. As you rely on Him in faith, He will direct your steps along the road to a destination of His love, hope, and comfort.

Dear Lord,

Having cancer is not how I planned this year to be. It can be so confusing at times making decisions concerning my treatments and care. I hope I am making wise choices. What a relief to know that as I trust in You, You are guiding me each step along the way on this journey. Thank You for loving me.

In Jesus' name I pray, amen.

May your steps be sure and confident in God's love this year!

30

Thou Shalt Be a Stickler

Winning with God's Rules

*Blessed is the man who endures temptations;
for when he has been approved, he will receive the crown of life,
which the Lord has promised to those who love Him.*

~ James 1:12

Our grandchildren loved to play board games with us when they were younger. Monopoly Jr. was the game of choice on one of our visits. Our grandson hated to lose and began to make up the rules of the game to his advantage. After he ignored several admonishments, we stopped playing the game. Trying to manipulate the rules and ignore our instructions resulted in an unpleasant experience for all of us.

Later that day I played the same game with our granddaughter. She was a stickler for playing by the rules. When I would "accidentally" forget to collect my fee for passing Go, she quickly reminded me to pay myself from the bank. The result was a win for our granddaughter fair and square and a fun time for both of us.

Following the rules and instructions of a game makes playing with others more pleasurable. Following the rules and instructions given by God makes meeting the challenges of daily life more pleasurable, reassuring, and peaceful.

Many challenges confronted the Israelites on their exodus from bondage in Egypt. God gave divine instructions, the Ten

Commandments and Mosaic Law, to show them how to face the challenges more effectively while honoring God.

On the long difficult journey through the wilderness, the Israelites grew weary and discouraged, tempted to abandon God's rules and instructions and go forward following their own rules. But each time they did, they encountered more difficult challenges on the journey. And each time they were "sticklers" for following God's rules, they were blessed, strengthened, and encouraged to complete their journey.

At times of medical challenges, following rules and instructions are vitally important. During treatment for cancer we must carefully follow instructions and advice for medications, appointments, tests, therapy, and foods we eat. Adhering to instructions makes the journey with cancer a little easier and more effective.

Following medical advice, rules and instructions of games, or the Ten Commandments, can sometimes seem restrictive and unpleasant. Like the Israelites, we may grow weary and discouraged during the long difficult journey and be tempted to change the rules or ignore instructions to achieve temporary satisfaction. But it will ultimately bring unpleasant and ineffective results.

Whatever challenges you may be facing with cancer, be a "stickler" for playing by the rules and instructions from your doctors and medical staff. Be a "stickler" for looking to God for strength and encouragement to endure unpleasant challenges and complete your journey with cancer. The result is a win for you of peace and reassurance in God's loving presence.

Dear God,

I know I must follow all the medical advice and instructions for the most effective treatment to this cancer, but some days I don't feel like it. Please give me the strength to be a stickler and endure the challenges on the difficult days. Thank You for helping me complete this journey.

In Jesus' name I pray, amen.

31

MAY ALL YOUR WISHES COME TRUE

The Power of Faith in Times of Need

*What man is there of you,
if his son asks him for a loaf of bread, will hand him a stone?
Or if he asks for a fish, will hand him a serpent?*
~ Matthew 7:9–10

In Jesus' day people asked him for bread and fish because they were staples, necessities of daily living. Jesus used everyday examples like bread and fish to teach His disciples and the people who followed Him about asking for their daily needs from the Heavenly Father.

Bread and fish are not what I would expect our grandchildren to ask from their parents. I would expect them to ask and ask and ask for what they think is a necessity to relieve their hunger—a pizza and a coke. Instead, their parents would probably give what they believe to be a good and advantageous necessity, such as a sandwich and a glass of milk.

We may not always perceive accurately what our necessities are, so we too might ask for pizza and a coke, instead of a loaf of bread and a fish. This is especially true when we have been diagnosed with cancer. It can be a confusing, emotional time. We know we have needs, but we may have difficulty perceiving exactly what those needs are or how to ask for those needs to be met in our hearts, minds, spirits, and daily routines. All we may know to do is ask for pizza and a coke.

Go ahead, ask. When we confidently come to the Father as His children and ask and ask and ask in faith, Jesus said that He will give us more good and advantageous things, the "bread and fish" we really need to nourish our spirits and take us daily through this journey with cancer.

> *If you then, evil as you are, know how to give* **good and advantageous gifts to your children,** *how much more will your Father Who is in heaven [perfect as He is] give* **good and advantageous things to those who keep on asking Him!**
> ~ *Matthew 7:11*

Heavenly Father,

Since I was diagnosed with cancer, every day I seem to wake up with a different need. Sometimes I don't know what to ask; I just know I need. Thank You that You already know what my need is. You are waiting for me to ask, so I am asking. I know it may not be pizza and a coke, but I am trusting You to give me what I need today.

In Jesus' name I pray, amen.

32

FEELING WEARY?

Consider the Dragonfly

*Do not become weary or lose heart in doing right
but continue in well-doing without weakening.*

~ 2 Thessalonians 3:13

The dragonfly spends the first years of its active life as larva. During that time (1–5 years), it undergoes a series of molts as it grows and develops. At the end of the last larval stage, it splits its skin open and pulls itself out through the hole. During this process it is vulnerable to wind, rain, other insects, and predators. Emergence into its new life requires a lot of energy, but the dragonfly perseveres.

The life of an adult dragonfly also requires incredible energy. It beats its wings more than 30 times per second and has been known to fly as fast as 60 miles per hour. It can fly forward and backward in darting motions, which assists it in feeding on insects and avoiding predators. Does a dragonfly feel weary? Perhaps, but it continues each day in "well-doing" through all its challenges.

We can feel exhausted and discouraged at times throughout our journey with cancer. We are not able to continue our normal routines of "well-doing" for our family and friends. Appointments, tests, treatments, and all their side effects drain our physical and emotional energies. Yet the Scripture encourages us to "not become weary or lose heart."

How can we continue in "well-doing" when we feel worn down and are unable to maintain our usual activities? Each day we persevere through all the challenges of our illnesses, we are "well-doing." As we pray and seek God, He will give us the strength we need to persevere throughout our journey.

So keep beating your wings!

Dear God,

I do feel weak and weary on this journey. I get tired of waking in the morning knowing I must schedule my day around another appointment. Needle sticks, treatments, and tests wear me out. Just wondering how I am going to feel tomorrow drains my energy. Most of all, I get discouraged worrying about being a burden to my family because I can't do what I normally would for them.

Help me to accept their help during this time and focus my energy on me—doing what I must to complete this journey. Thank You for good days. Strengthen me when I tend to "lose heart" on bad days, and help me to remember that I am "well-doing" each day by taking care of myself.

In Jesus' name, I pray. Amen.

Lord, I ask

Living Confidently
IN HIS STRENGTH

33

He's Got the Whole World *in* His Hands

*In his hand is the life of every living thing
and the breath of all mankind.*

~ Job 12:10

"He's got the whole world in His hands . . ." Do you remember that song from several years ago? The next verse began, "He's got the little bitty baby in His hands . . ." I used to sing my own version of that song when we got our little Chihuahua.

At six weeks old, she weighed only 14 ounces. We named her Peque, short for *el perro muy pequeno*, which is Spanish for "the very small dog." I carried her in the pocket of my bathrobe in the morning when I went downstairs and put her in a basket to carry around with me throughout the day. We could easily hold her in one hand. As I held and cuddled her, the song came to me, "I've got little bitty Peque in my hands . . ." She snuggled peacefully in my hands, completely trusting in my care of her life.

Now at six pounds Peque snuggles into my arms, sighs with a big breath, and contently goes to sleep. Sometimes when I am feeling overwhelmed by the stresses of the day, I look at Peque resting serenely and think, "I would like to trade places and be held and taken care of like you."

Living Confidently in His Strength

At times during my illnesses with cancer, when weariness and sickness overwhelmed me, all I had the strength to do was look to God for help and pray, "Just hold me." And God did, as He continues to do every day, teaching me to completely trust in His care for my life and breath.

Do you feel weary and overwhelmed on your journey with cancer? Take a deep breath and snuggle peacefully in God's hands. You can completely trust God to faithfully strengthen and care for you. He's got your life and breath in His hands.

As the song goes, "He's got you and me, brother, in His hands; He's got you and me, sister, in His hands. He's got the whole world in His hands."

Dear God,
Just hold me today.
In Jesus' name I pray,
Amen.

May you feel God's peaceful strength holding you today.

34

GOOD NIGHT SLEEP TIGHT

*Comforting Rest
in the Safe Cradle of God's Arms*

*In peace I will lie down and sleep,
for you alone, Lord, make me dwell in safety.*

~ Psalm 4:8

Many health specialists consider lack of sleep to be a major problem affecting our body's ability to deal with stress or fight off illness. Mattress companies promise we can have a restful night's sleep on their patented designs. Drug companies promise that we will sleep soundly and wake up refreshed by taking one of their pills.

Nevertheless, a diagnosis of cancer can disrupt our sleeping patterns, as we toss and turn over worry and concern about our illness. Then, as treatments and medications cause us to feel fatigued and weakened, we sleep more than normal. We sleep when we don't want to and can't sleep when we do want to.

As I was thinking about this and how Psalm 4:8 relates to our sleeping difficulties, my cat jumped up on my desk. He sniffed around the research books that lay scattered, stretched out on top of them, and settled in for a nap. My little Chihuahua then jumped up in my lap, squirmed around, snuggled into my arms, and closed her eyes for her nap. Although not their usual soft, warm napping spots (the middle of the bed and my husband's

Living Confidently in His Strength

easy chair), my cat and dog chose to sleep near me, assured of my presence keeping them safe.

Has the diagnosis of cancer disrupted your usual sleeping pattern? During those times when all you feel like doing is to sleep, it's okay. Lie down, stretch out in peace, and sleep. Get the rest your body needs. When you toss and turn and sleep will not come, it's okay. Squirm around and snuggle into the cradle of Father God's arms; then rest in the assurance of his presence keeping you safe.

Good night, sleep tight!

Father God,

I know proper rest is important right now as I face treatment for cancer, but sometimes it's hard. I don't have peace. Help me to have the assurance that it is okay to snuggle into Your arms any time, and You will help me get the rest I need. Thank You for Your presence keeping me safe along this journey.

In Jesus' name, amen.

May you have many peaceful nights.

35

Looking Good

God's Encouraging Purpose

He has made everything beautiful in its time.
~ Ecclesiastes 3:11

With tubes hanging from her thin chest, a sick, yellow paleness and bald head highlighted a large scar from a recent mastectomy. Was this me? Six months into my chemotherapy, the image staring back from the mirror held little resemblance to the person I had looked at before. It seemed this was not a time God chose to make everything beautiful. Or was it?

I did not understand it at the time, and my outward appearance did not show it, but God was working out His divine purpose *within* me. Verse 11 of Ecclesiastes continues:

He also has planted eternity in men's hearts and minds
[a divinely implanted sense of a purpose working through the ages
which nothing under the sun but
God alone can satisfy] [1]

As I write this, my hair has grown back, my weight has returned (alas!), and there are no more tubes. I hope that along with the return of a healthy physical appearance, my inward beauty has grown and blossomed according to God's purpose.

Living Confidently in His Strength

I pray that my life now reflects what the Apostle Peter describes:

*Do not let your adornment be merely outward, ...
rather let it be the hidden person of the heart,
with the incorruptible beauty of a gentle and quiet spirit,
which is very precious in the sight of God.*[2]

You may not feel very attractive sometimes during your course of treatments. You may wonder if there is any purpose for what you are going through. You may question where God is during this time.

He is right there working out His divine purpose *within* you. Trust Him to give you a pleasing, gentle, quiet spirit that He alone can satisfy. You are very precious in God's sight, and He will make you beautiful in His time.

Dear God,

Some days I feel like an ugly old worm as I go through this process. It is encouraging to know You see me as beautiful. Help me to trust that You have something wonderful planned just for me, and You are working in me each day to fulfill Your special purpose for this time in my life.

In Jesus' name I pray, amen.

You're looking good today.

36

COME AND SEE

See the Abundant Strength within the Works of God

> Come and see the works of God.
> ~ Psalm 66:5

"Everything looks so beautiful," my husband said as we relaxed on our patio gazing over our backyard on an early, warm summer day. Bright yellow blossoms blended with brilliant red, soft pink, iridescent purple, and blazing white flowers to paint a colorful backdrop for the luscious green lawn. We strolled over to inspect our garden looking full and flourishing after abundant spring rains. It was easy to "see the works of God."

Later in the summer, however, the works of God were not so easy to see. The ground was parched and cracked from drought. A few hardy flowers still displayed spots of color, but the plants in our garden were wilted and withered. We did not see the beauty of God's works until we learned two lessons from zucchini and peas.

LESSON ONE: On top of withered leaves lay a two-foot zucchini. The lush green growth of early summer had hidden this bounty. Only when the leaves withered from the drought were we able to "see the works of God!"

Lesson Two: Useless and unappetizing pea pods filled the bowl until the sweet bounty within was revealed. They had to be broken open for us to "see the works of God!"

The lessons from our garden made me think about my illness with cancer. My life was full and flourishing before the drought of cancer came along. I wilted and withered from tests, surgeries, treatments, and check-ups. I felt broken from the emotional drain of feeling useless and unproductive. It was sometimes difficult to "see the works of God."

This is what I have learned:

Lesson One: It is when we are wilted and withered, no longer dependent on lush full growth covering our lives, that we are able to see God at work strengthening and comforting us through our journey with cancer.

Lesson Two: It is when we are emotionally broken open that we are able to see God at work producing sweet bounty within us.

Dear God,

Cancer has created a physical and emotional barren drought in my life. Some days I feel wilted and withered like the plants. My emotions pull and tear at me leaving me feeling broken. Help me to see Your works during this season—to feel Your strength and comfort and to know the sweet bounty You are producing within me. Thank You for being with me.

In Jesus' name I pray, amen.

May the works of God produce
an abundant bounty of strength and comfort for you.

37

Just Hanging Around

Holding on to Godliness

Godliness with contentment is great gain.
~ I Timothy 6:6

On a warm summer evening, we sat on the deck and watched our grandchildren play in the yard. Our granddaughter suddenly got very excited and exclaimed, "I found a frog!" (Don't give her a doll. A frog is much better.) She ran into the house and came back with a washcloth. After carefully picking up the frog and gently wrapping it in her washcloth blanket, she cradled the frog (named Frog) lovingly close to her all evening. She frequently unwrapped Frog to gently stroke it and reassure it of her concern and care. As she spoke quiet loving words to it, Frog softly croaked back to her. Removed from its familiar secure environment, Frog appeared to peacefully endure its current circumstances and never struggled to get free.

When it was time to go in, we told our granddaughter to let Frog go back into the yard. Knowing that would be best for Frog, she gave Frog a soft kiss and carefully placed it back where she had found it. Frog did not move at first, but then hopped off looking content and quite unperturbed by the whole incident. Our granddaughter always remained watchful for Frog every time she was in the yard.

Living Confidently in His Strength

After being diagnosed with cancer for the third time and removed from my familiar secure environment, unlike Frog, I felt discouraged, afraid, and alone. Then God carefully picked me up, gently wrapped me in His arms, and lovingly carried me close, whispering words of hope and comfort, helping me peacefully endure my treatments. Discouragement, fears, and loneliness faded into contentment as I trusted in God's care.

When my treatments were over, He gave me a soft kiss. Knowing what was best for me, He let me go to a new life after cancer, while remaining ever watchful over me.

You, too, can peacefully endure the circumstances of cancer. When you are feeling discouraged, afraid, or alone, look to God with trust and hope. In His arms you will experience comfort and contentment, assured that God knows what is best for you and will keep you in His watchful love and care. That is great gain!

Dear Lord,

Pick me up, wrap me in Your arms, carry me close, and encourage me as only You can. Help me to stay content in the assurance that You know what is best for me, even on my most difficult days. Thank You for watching over me during this cancer journey.

In Jesus' name I pray, amen.

---

*Remember, you can **Forever Rely On God**.*

38

Yum!

Satisfied with God's Abundant Blessings

*You shall eat in plenty and be satisfied,
and praise the name of the Lord your God.*

~ Joel 2:26

My mother always said there was something wrong with my two brothers and me. Jelly beans that she set out would ruin before we ate it all. A few pieces satisfied us. As a candy lover, my mother could never understand that. When some of my friends came over, however, she had to hide the candy as they would eat in plenty until satisfied.

During the rough challenging times when I am in treatment for cancer, I desire to be able to eat in plenty and be satisfied. Food does not agree with my nauseated stomach, or it tastes like cardboard, or the sores in my mouth make eating a joyless chore. Today, with treatments behind me, I eat in too much plenty and am too satisfied.

The ancient Israelite people faced some very difficult devastating situations, challenged by attacks from their enemies, captivity, deprivation, and even starvation. The Lord wanted His people to know He would bless them when they turned to Him with dependent trust, so He sent a message through the prophet Joel to encourage them about their future.

You may be going through some tough, demanding times with cancer. The Lord wants you to know He understands what you are enduring. Trust and rely on Him. He is your Giver of abundant blessings and will bless you, so you will *eat in plenty and be satisfied* (even jelly beans). Praise the name of the Lord!

Dear Lord,

Thank You for jelly beans that remind me of Your promise to be my refuge through this time. I will trust You, and when I eat, I will praise You for Your blessings.

In Jesus' name I pray, amen.

Jelly Bean Facts

- The origin of jelly beans dates back to biblical days with a Turkish candy made of soft jelly covered in confectioner's sugar. They first became known as jelly beans in 1861 when Boston confectioner William Schrafft urged people to send his jelly beans to soldiers during the Civil War.
- Most jelly beans are about the size of a red kidney bean or a baby kangaroo.
- Jelly beans are often used to screen pregnant women for gestational diabetes. Asked to consume 18 jelly beans in two minutes, the woman's blood sugar level is tested to see if it falls within a healthy range.
- President Ronald Reagan's favorite candy, Jelly Belly, debuted a new blueberry flavor in 1981 to commemorate his inauguration. A portrait of Ronald Reagan made from 10,000 Jelly Belly beans hangs in the Ronald Reagan Library.
- Professed to be low-calorie, smaller jelly beans contain little or no fat with about 150 calories in 2 tablespoons of beans.

- The process of making jelly beans takes 6 to 12 days, depending on the size and manufacturer. The process generates very little waste.
- Some manufacturers package and sell imperfectly shaped but edible beans; Jelly Belly sells theirs under the name of Belly Flops.
- Enough Jelly Belly beans were eaten in the last year to circle the earth more than five times. That's a lot of jelly beans—enough to "eat in plenty and be satisfied"!

Praying you have many satisfying days of plenty.

My Reflections

True Friends
ARE FOREVER!

39

FEELING ALONE?

Rest in the Refuge of God's Faithfulness

And God [earnestly] remembered Noah and every living thing and all the animals that were with him in the ark.

~ Genesis 8:1

His neighbors gathered around to stare and gawk, unable to understand his motivation and the importance of his work. Shaking their heads and shrugging their shoulders, they mumbled to themselves, expressing their opinions as they walked away. Noah and his sons were left alone to complete the task of building the ark. One hundred twenty years later, they finished, "*and the Lord shut him in and closed [the door] round about him.*"[1]

Shut away from the life they had known, Noah and his family waited alone in the ark. For seven days they pondered, perhaps in fear, the uncertainty of their tomorrows. Suddenly, in a tumultuous upheaval "*all the fountains of the great deep were broken up and burst forth, and the windows and floodgates of the heavens were opened.*"[2]

For five long months as the floodwaters engulfed the earth, "*the ark went [gently floating] upon the surface of the waters.*"[3] Although secure within the confines of the ark, Noah must have felt very alone during those long uncertain days and nights, while life on earth ceased to exist. But Noah wasn't alone, for God *remembered*

Noah and his family, not casually or fleetingly, but earnestly, sincerely, and intently.

Noah's name means "rest" or "relief." In spite of any feelings of uncertainty and loneliness Noah may have felt, he trusted God to remember him and provide rest and relief, as God brought him through the lonely trying times of building the ark and enduring the stormy flood.

Shut away from life as I had known it, I often felt alone during the trying stormy times of my three journeys with cancer. All the tests, surgeries, and treatments felt like tumultuous floodwaters threatening to engulf me. Although my family and friends gathered around to support me, I questioned, *Do they really understand my pain, my fears, and my uncertainties?* Yet, as I endured through the long days and nights and trusted in God, He "remembered" me. Gently floating within the secure refuge of God's presence, I found rest and relief when I needed it most.

Do you feel shut away and alone facing uncertain tomorrows with cancer? Trust God to bring you through the trying times of your journey. Just as he did with Noah and with me, He will gently wrap you within the secure refuge of His presence, providing the rest and relief you need.

You are not alone. God remembers you—earnestly, sincerely, intently remembers you.

Dear God,

Thank You for the assurance that You are watching over me, especially during lonely, stormy times. Through all the uncertainties of this journey, help me to remember that You are remembering me.

In Jesus' name I pray, amen.

40

HEAVEN IS WATCHING OVER YOU

I will not leave you comfortless:
I will come to you.

~ John 14.18

Country comedian Archie Campbell enjoyed telling about two sweethearts who were sitting on the front porch. The young man noticed that tears were streaming down his girlfriend's face. He said, "What's the matter with my little sweetheart? I'll kiss those tears away."

After kissing a few times, he noticed she was still crying. He said, "Won't anything stop those tears?"

She said, "It's hay fever, darling, but keep up the treatment."[1]

What brings tears to your eyes and makes you cry? Hay fever, a sad movie, problems with your children, stories of war, the diagnosis of cancer or a serious illness? Tears came when I was diagnosed with cancer. Tears came on the first day of treatment. Tears came in the middle of treatments. Tears came toward the end of treatments. In fact, tears came many times during the journey. I have noticed that although I am now in remission, tears come much more easily these days.

The Bible tells us there is *"a time to weep."*[2] The shedding of tears is recorded throughout the Bible. Jeremiah, known as the weeping prophet, compared his weeping to a *"fountain of tears."*[3]

During a time of anguish, the psalmist David lamented, *"All night long I flood my bed with weeping and drench my couch with tears."*[4] Peter, after denying Christ three times, *"wept bitterly."*[5] Jesus himself felt emotions that caused Him to weep with His friends at the death of Lazarus[6] and to weep over a doomed city.[7] The last mention of tears in the Bible is the promise that God will wipe away all tears from the eyes of His redeemed.[8]

Our tears are important to God. Psalm 56:8 tells us He keeps track of all our sorrows. *"Record my misery; list my tears on your scroll—are they not in your record?"*[9] He understands all the emotions that bring tears because of a cancer diagnosis. As we turn to Him with our tears, Jesus promises,

> *I will not leave you comfortless:*
> *I will come to you.*

Now that's true friendship.

Dear God,

I have tried to be brave and not cry since I heard that I have cancer, but sometimes I can't stop the tears. I am comforted knowing that it's okay to cry, that You love me so much You catch each one of my many tears. Help me to lean on You as I go through this journey.

In Jesus' name I pray, amen.

May Jesus wipe away all your tears.

41

Friends Share the Joy *and* Divide the Sorrow

*Rejoice with those who rejoice,
and weep with those who weep.*

~ Romans 12:15

Diane and I connected instantly when we learned we both had breast cancer. I was recovering from recent chemotherapy, and Diane was in her fifth year of treatment for metastatic breast cancer. We enjoyed getting together to refresh ourselves with some lemonade in the summer or hot chocolate in the winter, and giving each other updates on our progress. We rejoiced when Diane shared the good news that her cancer markers had remained stable and her oncologist was decreasing the chemotherapy treatments. We rejoiced when I shared that my oncologist had promoted me to six-month intervals between checkups.

One day Diane called and cried, "My recent CAT scan showed the cancer has spread into my ribs and liver." We met again for lemonade, but this time we wept together as Diane shared her feelings about preparing her family and her heart for going home to the Lord. The last time Diane and I met, I gave her a special mug that read, "Friends never say good-bye, just I'll see you again."

"I'm looking forward to sharing a heavenly cup of lemonade with you when I meet you again in heaven," I said, as we hugged and wept and rejoiced together one last time here on earth.

I wept over the temporary loss of my friend, and I rejoiced with Diane on her final victory over cancer. I hope I encouraged Diane on her journey. I know she was an encouragement to me as we shared our joys and sorrows.

I encountered many occasions of rejoicing and weeping through my three journeys with cancer. I wept over the initial shock and fear of the unknown, over uncertainties of treatments and their outcome, and wept from pain, worry, stress, and fatigue. I wept with others I encountered on the journey as we shared each others' sorrows and disappointments when results of tests and treatments did not produce the hoped for outcome.

Occasions of weeping were often laced with sparkles of rejoicing with my friends—rejoicing over positive test results, renewed strength and energy, completed treatments, or simply having a good day. Sharing times of rejoicing was encouraging and uplifting and made the journey a bit easier.

It is also made easier when we know our best friend, Jesus Christ, is rejoicing and weeping with us along the way. When we share our joys with Him, He illuminates them with the brightness of His love. When we share our sorrows with Him, He comforts and lifts us with hope for tomorrow.

Lord Jesus,

Some days I feel like weeping because of this diagnosis and what tomorrow may bring. Then I think about when You died on the cross and rose from the grave victorious over death. I have the promise of living eternally in Your home! I pray that the treatments will be successful. But whatever the outcome of this journey, help me to rejoice knowing I do not need to fear tomorrow because You are with me. You are my closest friend.

In Your name I pray, amen.

Look for sparkles of joy today. There is hope.

42

I'M HERE FOR YOU!

God's Encouraging Friendships

*To him who is afflicted,
kindness should be shown by his friend.*
~ Job 6:14

"I'm so sorry," my friend replied after I told her I had been diagnosed with breast cancer. I remembered her words of kindness many times during my treatments. Caring words and acts of kindness from a friend are a comfort on our journey with a serious illness like cancer.

Job longed for caring words and acts of kindness from his friends after the devastating loss of his health, family, fame, and fortune. The book of Job relates the narratives between Job and four of his friends as he tries to make them understand his suffering. However, although they had good intentions, instead of comfort they responded with critical counsel. Job pleaded with his friends to show pity and kindness instead of making him feel worse.

Some friends mean well and want to help but are uncomfortable with our diagnosis. They may be quick to give advice and make glib comments of "I understand" in their efforts to make us and themselves feel better.

Others seem to have a genuine understanding of pity and kindness. We depend on them to inquire about our welfare, listen to our grievances, and mingle their tears with ours. They say to us, "I don't understand why you are ill, but I will be here for you."

Like Job, we need the support of our friends through our trials. Thinking about special acts of kindnesses shown by friends helps make the discomforts of cancer a little easier to bear. And it will help us relate to them what we are going through and how they can best encourage us.

Remember, a friend is God's way of showing us we do not walk alone through our journey.

Dear God,

Thank you for the friends You send me. I especially need their friendship and support now. Help me to be patient with them when they don't seem to really understand what I am going through, and give me wisdom how to communicate with them about my needs. Most of all, thank You for my best friend, Jesus, who understands everything I am feeling and cares.

In Jesus' name, amen.

---

*Praying a special touch of kindness for you today,
from your friend Jesus.*

Thank you, Lord, for my friends . . .

Keep Faith
ALIVE

43

THE POWER OF PRAYER *in* TIMES OF UNCERTAINTY

Lord, teach us to pray.
~ Luke 11:1

Three brief years was all the time Jesus had to teach His disciples lessons that would build their faith, enabling them to go and impact the world with the Gospel message. They witnessed Jesus heal, cast out demons, rebuke religious leaders, teach, and pray. Even though Jesus' teachings were frequently beyond their understanding, the disciples watched and marveled and questioned. Jesus patiently taught and explained as He prepared them for their missions after His crucifixion and resurrection.

Jesus' ministry was intense and exhausting. The disciples observed Jesus often retreating to quiet places to pray and refresh Himself. Yearning to emulate their Master, they asked Jesus, *"Lord, teach us to pray."* Jesus responded by teaching them a simple brief prayer that has been cherished over the centuries as a model and guide for powerful prayers of faith. We know it today as "The Lord's Prayer."

Do you have times when you want to pray but just don't know how to start or what to say? I do. Try using "The Lord's Prayer" as a guide to express your needs, your hurts, your desires, and your joys as you travel the road with cancer. He is waiting to hear from you.

Keep Faith Alive

Our Father which art in heaven, Hallowed be thy name.

Father, I know You are ever present, always ready to hear my prayers. I praise You and thank You for being the loving, compassionate God You are.

Thy kingdom come. Thy will be done in earth, as it is in heaven.

This journey with cancer has been hard, but I pray for Your perfect will to be accomplished through me and in me. Although I may not always understand Your purpose for what I am going through, I am trusting that You want only the best for me.

Give us this day our daily bread.

I need Your strength, Your wisdom, and Your courage to get through this journey. Please let me feel Your presence this day, holding me close, supplying all my needs.

And forgive us our debts, as we forgive our debtors.

I don't want anything to stand between us. Help me to let go of my feelings of anger and unforgiveness toward _____.

And lead us not into temptation, but deliver us from evil.

Cancer makes me feel weak and vulnerable. Cover me with Your protection from any attacks of the enemy. Help me to stand securely strong in Your faithful care.

For thine is the kingdom, and the power, and the glory, for ever.

Father,

You are my strength and comfort for today and my hope for tomorrow.

In Jesus' name I pray, amen.

My Pilgrimage Devotional

Lord, hear my prayer . . .

Our Father which art in heaven, Hallowed be thy name.

Thy kingdom come. Thy will be done in earth, as it is in heaven.

Give us this day our daily bread.

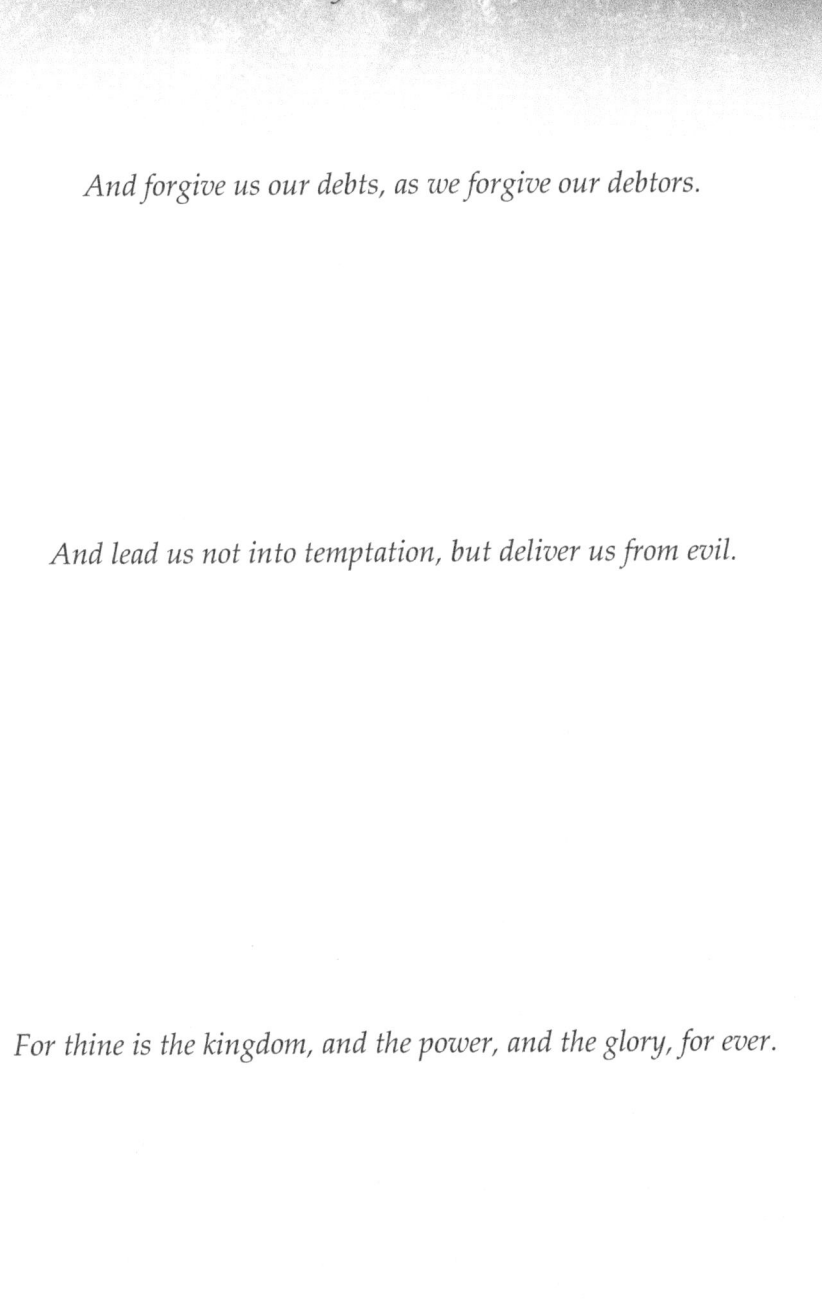

And forgive us our debts, as we forgive our debtors.

And lead us not into temptation, but deliver us from evil.

For thine is the kingdom, and the power, and the glory, for ever.

44

TREASURES OF THE SNOW

Secure in God's Sovereign Warmth

*Hast thou entered into the treasures of the snow? . . .
Which I have reserved against the time of trouble.*
~ Job 38:22–23

I love snow, as long as I don't have to drive in it! It brings out the child in me. I grew up in southeastern New Mexico where everyday life came to a stop for 3–4 inches of snow that lasted for a day. So the Christmas of 2004 in Ohio was very surreal to me—18 inches of snow. Wow! Like two overgrown children, my husband and I laughed and giggled as we played in the snow building a snowman and throwing snowballs at each other. We were surprised that I (who grew up in the desert) taught my husband (who grew up in the Snowbelt near Pittsburgh) how to make snow angels and snow ice cream. After we had "entered into the treasures of the snow," we thawed out in front of the fireplace, warm, secure, and at peace.

Unfortunately, the winter snowstorm brought cold, insecurity, and a time of trouble to many that Christmas. Some travelers were stranded and had to spend Christmas apart from their families. Others were confined in their homes, some without electricity and heat for several days.

Where were the treasures of the snow?

Where are the treasures of the snow when we are diagnosed with cancer, when we feel cold, stranded, and troubled?

Where is God?

That's how Job felt after he had lost the warmth of his family, the security of his business, and the peace of good health. So he questioned God,[1] and God responded by taking Job on a tour of His creation through a series of rhetorical questions: *"Where were you when I laid the earth's foundation?" "Have you ever given orders to the morning, or shown the dawn its place?" "Have you journeyed to the springs of the sea or walked in the recesses of the deep?" "Does the eagle soar at your command and build his nest on high?"*[2]

Confronted by the sovereignty and majesty of God, the Creator and Sustainer, Job realized that God was in full control through his time of trouble. In humility and relief he responded to God, *"I know that you can do all things; no purpose of yours can be thwarted . . . Surely I spoke of things I did not understand, things too wonderful for me to know."*[3]

We, too, can surrender in relief during our times of trouble with cancer in the realization that when we enter into the treasures of the snow and humble ourselves before God, we find warmth, security, and peace knowing that He is in full control.

Dear God,

You are too great and marvelous to understand all Your ways. I don't understand why I have this illness, but I am humbled knowing that You will keep me warm through my time of trouble wrapped in Your love, hope, and comfort.

In Jesus' name I pray, amen.

45

WHAT DID I FORGET
to REMEMBER?

Reassuring Relief in the Palms of God's Hands

I will not forget you!
~ Isaiah 49:15

It's chemo brain again, I sighed to myself. I smiled a friendly greeting and tried to remember who the lady was that had called my name in the aisle at WalMart.

"It's so good to see you. How are you doing?" she asked.

Who is she? Where do I know her from? What is her name?

"I want to thank you again for all the cards you gave me while I was in chemo. They really helped me get through the rough times," she said as she continued to recall some of her experiences during chemotherapy. *Aha! I know her from the oncology clinic. But what is her name?*

"You probably don't remember me. My name is Gwen."

"Oh yes, of course I remember," I replied with relief as glimmers of remembrance tickled my brain. "I didn't recognize you at first. You have hair now!" We both laughed and exchanged well wishes for continued good health before going our separate ways.

Although my last chemotherapy treatment was in April of 1999, chemo brain has become a convenient excuse when I cannot remember something. I find I am using it more frequently these days. *What did I come downstairs for? What was on my shopping list that I forgot to pick up when I left home? What was the name of that special treat we like at Christmas?*

Determined to help out my chemo brain, I tried carrying a note pad around the house and in my purse. The note pad ended up being forgotten at the last place I laid it down.

I guess I should resort to using my father's method of remembering—the palms of his hands. He never carried a note pad but always had a good pen ready to whip out of his pocket and jot down on his open palm someone's name, a phone number, or measurements. His information remained safe and secure in his hand until he got to his desk to write it down on paper.

We can joke about our forgetfulness, but it is no joke when we wonder if God has forgotten us. That was how I felt during some of the rough times of my chemotherapy treatments. *Has God forgotten me?* Do you feel that way, too, sometimes during your illness? God has a reassuring message for us:

> *I will not forget you!*
> *See, I have engraved you on the palms of my hands.*
> ~ Isaiah 49:15–16[1]

Be encouraged. God does not have chemo brain, nor does He need note pads. He has never forgotten you and never will. He will faithfully keep you safe and secure in the palms of His hands when you trust in His Son Jesus Christ.

Dear God,

Thank You that You have preserved in Your Word this Scripture just for me just for today. When I look at my hands, help me to remember that You care for me so much You engraved me in the palms of Your hands. What an encouragement!

In Jesus' name I pray, amen.

46

LIBERTY

Winning with Liberating Love

*Stand fast therefore in the liberty
by which Christ has made us free.*

~ Galatians 5:1

We live in a country where freedom is a way of life. Too often we take it for granted; that is, until a serious illness like cancer invades your life. Simple everyday freedoms must be put aside as you undergo treatments and experience the limitations of cancer. Cancer need not, however, rob the freedom of your spirit.

Cancer cannot quench the power of the liberating love of Christ for you. His love frees you from fear over tomorrow, from worry over your family, from sadness over the losses cancer has caused, and frees you from anger over the unfairness of this illness.

The liberating love of Christ frees you to trust in His unfailing care over you, to depend on His strength, to follow His wisdom and guidance, to experience His peace that passes all understanding, to smile, to laugh, and to cry.

The liberating love of Christ frees you to have courage and confidence for today and to have faith and hope for tomorrow.

Keep Faith Alive

Dear God,

I have lost the freedom to do many things since cancer invaded my life. Thank You for all the freedoms You give me because of Your Son, Jesus Christ. I will stand fast in Your liberating love over me.

In Jesus' name I pray, amen.

My Reflections

47

KEEP THE FAITH

Trusting in God's Steadfast Love

*Let me hear in the morning of your steadfast love,
for in you I trust.*

~ Psalm 143:8

What does *trust* mean to you? Synonyms for trust include believe, hope, rely on, depend on, lean on, have confidence in, be certain about, remain steadfast, have faith in. Do you rely and depend on family and friends? Do you have confidence in your doctors? Were you certain the chair you are sitting on would hold you when you sat down? Do you believe and have faith that God will be with you through this journey with cancer?

Abraham, a patriarch of faith, encountered many occasions when he had to trust the Lord. *"Now the Lord had said to Abram: 'Get out of your country, from your family and from your father's house, to a land that I will show you.' So Abram departed as the Lord had spoken to him."*[1] (Abram's name was later changed to Abraham.)

There is no mention of Abram's emotional response at being directed to suddenly leave his home and family for an uncertain future in an unknown land. Was he fearful, resentful, or unsure? The Bible only says that he *departed*. What a statement of trust! Abram must have set out with hope and faith completely relying and depending on God for his daily and future needs.

Later as Abram aged, he despaired because he had no children by his wife Sarah. In a vision the Lord assured him that his descendants through Sarah would be as numerous as the stars in the sky. *"And he believed in the Lord."*[2]

Abram, now called Abraham, had to remain steadfast in his belief and trust; many years later in his and Sarah's old age, she bore him God's precious Isaac, the seed of God's promise to make him *exceedingly fruitful*.[3] This promised son became the ultimate test of Abraham's trust when God told him to sacrifice Isaac on an altar.

The Bible does not share with us any turmoil of emotions Abraham may have experienced, only that he *"rose early in the morning and saddled his donkey."*[4] With his son carrying the wood for the burnt offering, they traveled up to the place God had told them. Isaac asked his father, *"Where is the lamb for a burnt offering?"*[5] In confident trust *Abraham said, "My son, God will provide for Himself the lamb for a burnt offering."*[6]

Were tears streaming down his cheeks as he laid Isaac on the altar, while still believing in God's promise? Were his hands trembling as he held the knife above Isaac, hoping for God's salvation? An Angel of the Lord then intervened and showed Abraham a ram caught in a thicket nearby for the offering. Because of Abraham's faithful steadfast trust, God reassured him of His promise, *"blessing I will bless you, and multiplying I will multiply your descendants as the stars of the heaven."*[7]

In spite of any fears or doubts Abraham may have felt, with dependent trust he was willing to lay all that was most precious to him on the altar, relying on God's faithful loving provision. What do you need to put on an altar to God—plans for an uncertain future to an unknown destination on your journey with illness, concern for your family, or fear, anxiety, and confusion? Just as He faithfully took care of Abraham in each situation, God will lovingly take care of you as you believe and hope in, rely and depend on, and have steadfast faith and confidence in Him.

You can *trust* in the Lord!

Dear God,

I pray for my journey with cancer, *"Let me hear in the morning of your steadfast love, for in you I trust. Make me know the way I should go, for to you I lift up my soul."*[8]

In Jesus' name, amen.

My Reflections

Hugs & Hope
FOR THE HOLY HOLIDAYS

48

MAY CHRISTMAS HUG YOUR HEART

Did Christmas Hug Mary's heart?

Thanks be to God for his indescribable gift!
~ 2 Corinthians 9:15

The angels returned to heaven after delivering to the shepherds the message of good news that a Savior, Christ the Lord, had been born. With excitement the shepherds hurried to find the manger in Bethlehem. When they had seen him, they spread the word concerning what had been told them about this child, and all who heard it were amazed at what the shepherds said to them. But Mary treasured up all these things and pondered them in her heart.[1]

Mary already knew the baby she hugged to her heart was a special gift from God. An angel had visited her at the time of conception, and now she was told that an angel with *"a great company of the heavenly host"*[2] had announced his birth. Luke tells us she pondered these things in her heart.

To ponder means to think or consider quietly, soberly, and deeply. How will He be great? When will God give Him the throne of His father David? When will He reign over His kingdom that will never end?[3]

I wonder, did this first Christmas hug Mary's heart?

A popular Christmas song relates the events of the life of Jesus and each time asks, as she held the baby, "Mary, did you know?" Did Christmas hug her heart with each event?

I wonder as Mary watched her Son die on the cross if she remembered when she first held her infant Son.

Did Christmas hug her heart?

I wonder when Mary learned that her Son had triumphantly risen from the dead if she remembered the things she had pondered in her heart when He was first born.

Did Christmas hug her heart?

Does Christmas hug your heart during the events of your journey with cancer?

Like Mary, ponder the message of the Christ Child—a message of the peace and joy, and the hope and promise of Emmanuel, God with us, who will save His people from their sins, providing a way into His eternal Kingdom.[4]

Whether newly diagnosed with cancer, currently in treatment, facing an uncertain prognosis, or on the road to recovery, be encouraged by the promise that you can be a part of His Kingdom now and eternally when you hug Christ the Lord in your heart.

Dear Jesus,

So many things always hug my heart at Christmas time, but this year is different—this year cancer hugs my heart. But I want it to be different because of You. This year I want the love, hope, and comfort of the message of the Christ child to hug my heart. Thank You for the promise I have for tomorrow because of Christmas.

In Your name I pray, amen.

49

THE POWER
of the RESURRECTION

What Cancer Cannot Do

It cannot cripple Love.
It cannot shatter Hope.
It cannot corrode Faith.
It cannot destroy Peace.
It cannot weaken Confidence.
It cannot suppress Memories.
It cannot silence Courage.
It cannot invade the Soul.
It cannot quench the Spirit.
It cannot steal Eternal Life.
Cancer cannot lessen
The Power of the Resurrection!

~ Author Unknown

Jesus said to her, "I am the resurrection and the life. Whoever believes in me, though he die, yet shall he live and everyone who lives and believes in me shall never die."

~ John 11:25–26

Jesus, Thank you for the power of your resurrection. It gives me courage for today and hope for tomorrow. Amen.

My Reflections

50

TALE OF THREE TREES

Hope in God's Plan

*Surely there is a future,
and your hope will not be cut off.*
~ Proverbs 23:18

You may have heard this tale told in other contexts, but it also reveals deep insights to our journey with cancer:

Once upon a time, there were three little trees who all had a dream of what they would grow up to be someday.

Tree #1 hoped to be a beautiful treasure chest filled with gold, silver, and precious gems.

Tree #2 hoped to be a strong ship that would carry great kings and sail mighty waters.

Tree #3 hoped to grow straight and be the tallest tree in the forest. When people looked up at the tree, they would raise their eyes to heaven and think of God.

Time passed and one day three woodsmen came and cut down the three trees. They were made into something that was far from their dreams.

Tree #1 was made into a feed box for animals, not a beautiful treasure chest filled with great treasures.

Tree #2 was made into a small fishing boat, not a strong and mighty ship to carry great kings.

Tree #3 was made into long large beams and left alone in the dark, no longer a tall straight tree in the forest.

Many years passed by and the three trees almost forgot about each of their dreams, but God had not forgotten.

One starry night in a Bethlehem stable, Tree #1 held the greatest treasure in the world, Baby Jesus!

One evening, a great storm arose, and Tree #2 didn't think he would keep his passengers safe. Then one man who had been asleep in the boat arose and He calmed the storm. The tree knew he carried the King of kings across the waters.

Finally, Tree #3 was made into a rugged cross, and a man was nailed to it. High upon a hill, He died upon that cross. When Sunday morning came, the tree knew it was Jesus that had died for everyone upon the tree.[1]

They thought their dreams were forgotten, but God had a different plan to fulfill their dreams. God's plans are always best. Trust Him to show you His perfect way throughout your journey with cancer.

My Reflections

A Time to Give Thanks &
FOCUS ON A NEW YEAR

51

It's Thanksgiving

Full of God's Abundant Blessings

A faithful man will abound with blessings.
~ Proverbs 28:20

In 1977 I was undergoing chemotherapy treatments for Hodgkin's Disease. The drugs were very harsh and made me violently sick after each treatment. Medications were not available then as they are today to combat the sickness. I was scheduled for a treatment the day before Thanksgiving. Thinking about all the good food that I would not be able to enjoy made the dreaded treatment even harder. My mother planned a special menu of soft easily digestible food for me. Yuk!

We lived five hours from the cancer clinic in Albuquerque, New Mexico. After the treatment, feeling like the green color of the chemo chairs, I crawled onto the backseat of the car with my bucket and prepared for the long ride home and the oncoming sickness. We arrived home five hours later, and amazingly I felt wonderful. No sickness! The next morning I awoke hungry, ready to enjoy a full turkey dinner. Yum! This was the only time I experienced having no sickness from the treatments. What a blessing!

Thanksgiving time reminds us to focus on our blessings. It is not always easy to do when cancer has become the focus of our daily lives. Sometimes blessings are big and bold as they were with me that Thanksgiving of 1977. Most of the time, however, we must look a little harder to see the little blessings.

The Scripture says that we "abound with blessings" when we are faithful. Faithful how? As we are faithful in seeking God and talking to Him through prayer, He will show us the little blessings that He gives us in each day of our journey with cancer.

Some of my favorite little blessings include sunshine after dreary winter days, a warm comfortable bed when I am weary, a smile when I am down, my cat to greet me with his "Meow" when I come home. What a blessing!

What are your little blessings today?

Dear God,

I get so caught up in living each day with this cancer that I don't see the ways You bless me to let me know You are with me. Help me to see even the smallest blessing and enjoy the moment from You. Thank You for loving me.

In Jesus' name, amen.

Wishing you bountiful peace throughout your journey with cancer as you reflect upon God's blessings, His love, His Hope, and His comfort.

Thank you, Lord, for _____

52

It's a New Year

*Walk in wisdom toward outsiders,
making the best use of the time.*
~ Colossians 4:5

How do you feel about the New Year? Is it just a time to put up another new calendar as you continue on in the same manner as last year? Are you troubled and uncertain what the new year will bring with a cancer diagnosis? Or are you looking forward to the new year with hope and anticipation?

A few years ago as I filled my daily pillbox, I remember thinking, "At last! No more taking Tamoxifen to help prevent a recurrence of breast cancer." I reflected back over the past few years since I was diagnosed with cancer for the third time. At first my days were numbered one day at a time with each daily visit to the hospital for medication, then one week at a time with each doctor's appointment, then three months at a time for checkups, and then in six month blocks of time. I have now graduated to annual intervals of time between each checkup.

Each of these stages has marked a significant milestone in my journey with cancer. Hanging up my calendar for the new year marks another milestone, but the gift of every individual day is what I have learned to value. The Living Bible says in Psalm 90:12,

A Time to Give Thanks & Focus on a New Year

*Teach us to number our days
and recognize how few they are;
help us to spend them as we should.*

A diagnosis of cancer certainly teaches us to recognize how few our days are. It is a constant reminder to avoid complacency and apathy and to make the most of our days on earth.

But how do we avoid feeling troubled and uncertain about our days? By placing our hope and anticipation in our refuge, the Lord Jesus Christ, each day can be a unique and special blessing regardless of the circumstances with our illness.

He promises,

*Because of the Lord's great love we are not consumed,
for his compassions never fail.
They are new every morning;
great is your faithfulness.
I say to myself, "The Lord is my portion;
therefore I will wait for him."
The Lord is good to those whose **hope** is in him,
to the one who seeks him.*

~ Lamentations 3:22-25[1]

*But those who **hope** in the Lord
will renew their strength.
They will soar on wings like eagles;
they will run and not grow weary,
they will walk and not be faint.*

~ Isaiah 40:31[2]

May you soar this year with Jesus.

Dear Lord,

I don't know what to expect this new year with this diagnosis. But I look forward with hope and anticipation for Your love, compassion, and strength to cover me, so that I will not just walk and run but soar through each day of the year with You. Thank You for Your great faithfulness.

In Jesus' name I pray, amen.

My reflections for a new year

Epilogue

When Linda was going through her last bout with cancer, at one point I thought I had lost her. By God's grace she recovered. While she was hospitalized and enduring intensive treatment, I camped out with her and asked, "Linda, what would you enjoy doing if you had the opportunity?"

Much to my surprise she responded, "I would love to drive around the country, Joe, in one of those big trucks [18 wheelers]." We talked about what this might be like, and I told her I would give it serious consideration.

At the time I was a Realtor®. In 2008 when the housing and mortgage industry imploded, I told Linda if ever there were a time to change careers and start driving a big rig, it was now.

I went to truck driving school and after graduation found employment with a company in Missouri. After one year of experience I purchased my own truck, and Linda went with me two weeks at a time each month.

The truck had a conventional large body with two beds, a microwave, TV, and a converter so we could operate all electrical equipment. In 2010 I purchased my own trailer and obtained my own operating authority under the name Astron LLC, dba Astron Transport.

This allowed me to book my own loads and travel in the regions of my choice. When I booked a load to a location where we were close to sightseeing areas, we would park the truck after making our delivery and call Enterprise Rent-A-Car. They picked us up and took us back after we were done touring.

We visited many US areas from the Southeast to the great Northwest, from the plains to the Colorado Rockies (in summertime), from eastern cities to Salt Lake City, San Jose, and Albuquerque, to national sites like Mount Rushmore and Yellowstone National Park--and many more. We were even able to make stops in Linda's home town of Carlsbad, NM when travelling in the Southwest and visit with family and friends.

This was a dream come true for Linda. The trips gave her a time to rest, unwind, and reflect on the ministry. During this time she wrote more devotionals and started a new series of writings about life on the road with a trucker that may be published in the future.

On average we spent about ten hours on the road each work day. The first two days on the road, Linda would sleep a lot since I was either driving, loading, or unloading. Trucking is not an easy job, but the joy it gave her made every hour of work worthwhile.

We didn't originally plan to set foot in 48 states; however, we did. The last state we needed to complete our map was Rhode Island. Six months prior to the Lord taking Linda home, we made a delivery to our smallest state.

For 16 years, Linda victoriously fought the good fight with cancer, and it was not cancer that took her. Linda passed away January 15, 2014 from complications of Histoplasmosis Pneumonia. The Lord had another plan for her, and today Linda is joyful, healthy and whole, completely fulfilled in the Lord's presence.

I have since closed the business and sold the truck and trailer. My life's mission now is to continue Reflecting Light Ministry and Linda's dream of bringing God's light of comfort and hope into the hearts of those on their own pilgrimage with cancer and serious illness.

Acknowledgments

I, Joe Kovarik, first want to thank the God of Abraham, Isaac, and Jacob for the inspiration given to Linda to share her story. Thank you Jesus Christ and the Holy Spirit for empowering me to carry on Linda's ministry that touches the lives of those struggling in their own storms as pilgrims of cancer.

I thank my family for being there when I needed them, especially my son Joe and daughter Jodie.

Thanks to Bob & Dorothy Benz (Linda's brother and sister-in-law) for all your support during and after Linda's terminal illness.

Thank you Denise Olthaus, RN for opening the door to the Reflecting Light Ministry in the Oncology Clinic at McCullough-Hyde Memorial Hospital in Oxford, Ohio.

Thank you Richard Sunberg, Bonnie Arloski, and Judi Schuller for all your help with the card ministry.

Special thanks to the editors: Helen Rogers, Linore Burkard, and also Edie Glaser for her interior layout work and experience helping authors bring their books to market. Contact Edie at CraftingStones.com.

Thank you Lisa Hainline for designing the awesome book cover! You can contact Lisa at LionsGateBookDesign.com

Thank you Judy Miller for being a close friend to Linda and always willing to help with the ministry.

Thank you Middletown Area Christian Writers and Hamilton Writers Guild in Ohio. Also, thank you to so many others who helped along the way:

Martha Abarbanell	Alan & Diane Oak	Ellen Sippel
Cecelia Arrico	Denise Olthaus, RN	Sue Spires
Robin Atyeo	Judy Owens	Pastor Dianne Sloan
Marlene Benz	Peggy Rock	Pastor Johnny
Arnie Holm	Pastor Lee Rupert	Wade Sloan
Anna Kennedy	Roger & Phillis Richardson	Mary Thimons
Pastor Dan Knisley		Chaplain Joe Wargo
Vicky & Rob May	Pastor Bob Shallenberger	Mary Lou Curry
Don Moore		Ann Harnish

Scripture Notes

1. 2 Corinthians 5:17, NKJV
2. John 8:12, NIV
3. Matthew 5:44; (1) Luke 23:34, NKJV; (2) 2 Corinthians 12:10, NKJV; (3) Philippians 4:13, NKJV
4. Isaiah 40:26, NIV
5. Hebrews 10:23, NIV; Isaiah 41:13, NIV
6. 2 Corinthians 4:17, NIV (1) Romans 12:12, NIV; (1) 2 Corinthians 4:17, NIV
7. Psalm 17:8, NLT
8. 1 John 4:16, NIV; Jeremiah 31:3 NIV
9. 1 Samuel 16:7, NIV; (1) 1 Samuel 16:7, ESV; (2) 1 Samuel 16:12, ESV; (3) 1 Samuel 13:14, ESV
10. Psalm 8:3–5, ESV
11. All verses taken from NLT: (1) Zephaniah 3:17 (2) Matthew 10:30 (3) Psalm 73:26 (4) Job 12:10 (5) Jeremiah 29:11 (6) Proverbs 3:5 (7) 2 Corinthians 12:9 (8) Matthew 6:30
12. Proverbs 15:13, NKJV; (1) Romans 8:39, NKJV
13. Psalm 13:1–2, NKJV; (1) Psalm 13:5–6, NKJV
14. John 3:16–17, NIV
15. Isaiah 43:2, NLT; (1) Proverbs 24:3, AMP
16. Proverbs 3:5–6, NKJV; (1) Deuteronomy 31:6, ESV; (2) Psalm 32:8, ESV; (3) Matthew 6:31–32, ESV; (4) Jeremiah 24:6, ESV; (5) Proverbs 3:24, ESV; (6) Jeremiah 29:11, ESV
17. Isaiah 40:8, ESV; (1) Hebrews 4:12, NKJV
18. Genesis 15:1, ESV; (1) Exodus 3:14, ESV; (2) Genesis 15:1, ESV; (3) Genesis 28:15, ESV; (4) Isaiah 48:17, ESV; (5) Isaiah 51:12, ESV; (6) John 8:12, ESV; (7) John 11:25, ESV; (8) Matthew 28:20, NIV
19. John 14:27, NLT
20. Matthew 14:27, NLT; (1) Matthew 14:25, NLT; (2) Matthew 14:28–31, NLT

Scripture Notes

21. Psalm 46:1, NIV; (1) Psalm 119:114, NIV

22. Psalm 56:4, ESV; (1) Psalm 56:3, AMP

23. Psalm 42:11 NLT; (1) Genesis 4:5, ESV; (2) Genesis 4:3, ESV; (3) Genesis 4:12, ESV; (4) Exodus 32:19, ESV; (5) Isaiah 5:24–25, ESV; (6) Matthew 21:12–13, ESV; (7) Psalm 86:15–17, NLT

24. Philippians 4:6, NKJV; (1) Philippians 4:7, NKJV

25. Psalm 4:7, NKJV

26. Psalm 97:1, KJV

27. Psalm 113:3, MEV

28. James 1:22, NKJV; (1) Psalm 119:103, ESV; (2) Matthew 6:33, NLT (1996); (3) Philippians 4:6–7, NLT; (4) Proverbs 3:5–6, NLT; (5) Matthew 11:28, NLT; (6) I Peter 5:6, NLT; (7) 1 Corinthians 2:9, NLT

29. Proverbs 16:9, AMP

30. James 1:12, WEB

31. Matthew 7:9–10, AMP

32. 2 Thessalonians 3:13, AMP

33. Job 12:10, ESV

34. Psalm 4:8, NIV

35. Ecclesiastes 3:11, NKJV; (1) Ecclesiastes 3:11, AMP; (2) I Peter 3:3–4, NKJV

36. Psalm 66:5, NKJV

37. I Timothy 6:6, NKJV

38. Joel 2:26, ESV

39. Genesis 8:1, AMP; (1) Genesis 7:16, AMP; (2) Genesis 7:11, AMP; (3) Genesis 7:18, AMP

40. John 14.18, KJV; (1) Morgan, Robert J., *Stories, Illustrations, & Quotes* (Nashville: Thomas Nelson, 2000), 725. (2) Ecclesiastes 3:4, NIV; (3) Jeremiah 9:1, NIV; (4) Psalm 6:6, NIV; (5) Matthew 26:75, NIV; (6) John 11.35, NIV; (7) John 11:35; Luke 19:41, NIV; (8) Revelation 21:4, NLT; (9) Psalm 56:8, NIV

41. Romans 12:15, NKJV

42. Job 6:14, NKJV

43. Luke 11:1, ESV; The Lord's Prayer: Scriptures taken from Matthew 6:9–13, KJV

Scripture Notes

44. Job 38:22–23, KJV; (1) Job 31; (2) Job 38, 39, NIV; KJV (3) Job 42:2–3, NIV

45. Isaiah 49:15, NIV; Isaiah 49:15–16, NIV

46. Galatians 5:1, NKJV

47. Psalm 143:8, ESV; (1) Genesis 12:1, 4, NKJV; (2) Genesis 15:6, NKJV; (3) Genesis 17:6, NKJV; (4) Genesis 22:3, NKJV; (5) Genesis 22:7, NKJV; (6) Genesis 22:8, NKJV; (7) Genesis 22:17, NKJV; (8) Psalm 143:8, ESV

48. 2 Corinthians 9:15, NIV; (1) Luke 2:17–19; (2) Luke 2:13, NIV; (3) Luke 1:32–33; (4) Matthew 1:21, 23

49. John 11:25–26, ESV

50. Proverbs 23:18, ESV; (1) "Tale of Three Trees" (author unknown)

51. Proverbs 28:20, ESV

52. Colossians 4:5, ESV; (1) Lamentations 3:22-25, NIV; (2) Isaiah 40:31, NIV

My Reflections

My Reflections

My Reflections

My Reflections